IT'S
YOUR
FUNERAL

It's Your Funeral

WILLIAM L. COLEMAN

Tyndale House
Publishers, Inc.
Wheaton, Illinois

SCRIPTURE QUOTATIONS
FROM THE FOLLOWING VERSIONS
ARE USED BY PERMISSION OF THEIR PUBLISHERS:

NEW INTERNATIONAL VERSION
COPYRIGHT © NEW YORK INTERNATIONAL BIBLE SOCIETY, 1973

THE LIVING BIBLE
COPYRIGHT © 1971 TYNDALE HOUSE PUBLISHERS

LIBRARY OF CONGRESS CATALOG CARD NUMBER 78-68911
ISBN 0-8423-1828-3, PAPER
COPYRIGHT © 1979 WILLIAM L. COLEMAN. ALL RIGHTS RESERVED
FIRST PRINTING, OCTOBER 1979
PRINTED IN THE UNITED STATES OF AMERICA

Dedicated

to

Clint Petersen

CONTENTS

PREFACE
IT FEELS GOOD TO
TALK ABOUT IT

Congratulations! You have decided to discuss funerals. This could be one of the most satisfying ventures you'll encounter. Funerals can be meaningful and helpful when they are done thoughtfully. They can also be frustrating and shocking to those who have pretended the experience would never come to them.

Funeral practices are surrounded by myths. Since starting this book I have talked to many people about the subject. It has been interesting to see how much misinformation is circulating. Not that it is intentional. Actually most people have avoided the subject. Consequently, they get a few half-truths and an assortment of rumors. Because of this lack of facts, everyone suffers. The family, the funeral director, the minister—all are victimized by sensationalism and myths.

Most people are surprised when they find the truth about the law and embalming. The price of cremation after a viewing is not as cheap as imagined. A Christian view of the body can be much different than we had supposed. Organ transplants may be a good Christian service. Christ's outlook on flowers for funerals could be an eye-opener. The salaries of funeral directors may be lower than we thought. There is more than one way to have a final service; you may want to think over the options.

Often those making funeral arrangements are smothered with guilt feelings. They're in remorse about their treatment of the deceased person while he was alive. Possibly they think they contributed to his death. Now they have an added anxiety: can they guess how the person wanted to be buried? Maybe they had better do it up big to make up for previous failures.

Christians, of all people, should not be swallowed up in such a guilt trip. You can be a great help by letting the family know what kind of funeral you want. After all, it's your funeral.

William L. Coleman
Aurora, Nebraska

ACKNOWLEDGMENTS

Authors are not hard to recognize. Merely look for someone with a calendar in his pocket and a pen deeply imbedded in his hand. You'll notice that instead of standing erect he will be leaning on at least ten of his friends.

This author is no exception.

I want to thank the Aurora and Grand Island (Nebraska) Libraries for helping answer the strangest questions. Scores of people were kind enough to put up with my boorish inquiries.

John Thomas was an enormous help in discussing transplants.

The Wilbert Vault Company was kind enough to give me a copy of their survey and let me quote.

Congresswoman Virginia Smith, Senator Carl Curtis, and Senator Ed Zorinsky each did an excellent job of encouraging the Federal Trade Commission to send me material.

My sincere thanks goes to Jeanette Pickering of Lebanon, Missouri. The entire funeral industry should be proud of her.

James Higby and Ron Messman are two morticians who were willing to read the manuscript. Naturally they couldn't agree with everything I wrote. But such patience!

ONE
WHY CONSIDER IT NOW?

Today is a beautiful time to talk about dying. While we are healthy, alert and calm we can make death a wholesome, loving topic. The best way to remove some of its sting and shock is to face the subject maturely.

This sounds simple, but most people would rather ignore the inevitable. They are like travelers walking backward down a railroad track. There is no doubt a train will come sooner or later. They would rather not discuss it.

There is probably no way to make bereavement pleasant. When someone dies, he or she is ripped from our lives. No matter the circumstances or the person's age, it is similar to tearing away part of our body. The grief, pain, and shock are shattering. But usually those who have been willing to *discuss* death and funerals are able to meet these hardships with greater peace.

The major problem with funeral practices today is our refusal to discuss them. Read that sentence again. Our number one difficulty is not cost, viewing, transplants, or vaults. All such problems can be handled with considerable ease if we talk about them while we are healthy and happy.

"But why talk about something so morbid?" a young factory worker asked. "We have our whole life ahead of us. It all sounds so sad."

Discussing death and funerals doesn't have to be agonizing. When we acknowledge our mortality, life becomes more meaningful, not less. At the outside each of us has four- or five-score years, maybe considerably less. How do we want to live out our allotment and how do we want to end it?

The psalmist acknowledged his vulnerability and asked God to help him. "Teach us to number our days and recognize how few they are; help us to spend them as we should" (Psalm 90:12, TLB).

Death is probably years away for most of us. This should make it easier to discuss. Even if we expect to live for a century, it's not too early to talk about our personal preferences in arrangements.

For instance, have we considered the possibility of donating our organs? The best time to discuss the topic is now. The ideal place may be at a kitchen table with the whole family poring over literature. Myths can be erased and objections raised. The need can be evaluated and the honest odds weighed.

It is all so much better than hurried whispers in a hospital corridor at 2 A.M. Decisions are often misspent when heads and hearts are wracked with grief.

Certainly anyone who wants to depart seriously from the traditional funeral needs to prepare his family. Not only the immediate family but even the wider circle must be informed gently. If cremation is your preference it should be suggested as early as possible. The shock may be too much for those who aren't forewarned.

A minister sat with a family in Detroit and listened to a balanced conversation. The auto executive had conditioned his survivors for his funeral. He had spelled out carefully his personal preferences. In this case he wanted no radical changes from traditional practices. He had discussed his place of burial, taste in casket, choice of minister, and selection of hymns.

The family was at reasonable peace. While in good health he had outlined and explained his attitude toward death and funerals. His demands were within reach and no shock to his survivors.

If he could only have seen how much he had helped them! They were not left to guess or argue over the preparations. He spared them from added guilt feelings and bewilderment. They could say with confidence, "This is the way Dad wanted it. We're glad we could do it his way."

Basically a funeral is for the living. This tired but true slogan should be kept in our sights. When the individual outlines his choices he is doing a tremendous service for those who live on. He can take a heavy burden from their shoulders and reduce the uncertainty.

The individual who surprises his family with a bizarre plan borders on the cruel. Someone wants to be buried in a company packaging crate or some other crude plan. Has this person really considered the feelings of his family? In his selfishness he may have ignored the likelihood of heartache and embarrassment he would cause his survivors to suffer.

An ideal combination is the expression of some basic choices, coupled with reasonable leeway. The family needs some flexibility in case circumstances interfere. It is unwise to insist, for example, on a type of casket which might not be available at the time. The family's failure to supply the specified coffin would only give them guilt feelings. This is the last thing we want. In the case of cremation, the individual should keep his request for disposal of remains within sane boundaries.

For most it is safe to assume that we love our relatives. We have the opportunity to do a compassionate thing in our death. We do so by preparing them for our departure.

Unfortunately some people are overbalanced on the subject. They start to discuss death and soon become obsessed with the subject. It is a part of life; make preparation, revise occasionally, and forget about it.

Generally the problem is the other extreme. One man was asked if he had ever discussed his funeral with his wife. An otherwise congenial conversationalist, his face went stern and he became strangely quiet. At the first chance he abruptly changed the subject.

This kind of aversion is not uncommon. One person wants

nothing to do with the topic. He can't stand to visit anyone who is sick. He doesn't even want to hear about an illness. He knows he's mortal, yet he denies it. He'll die and yet he won't. Otherwise a practical realist, at this point he bails out. His family may someday wish he had confronted the facts.

If you find it difficult to discuss your own death and funeral, welcome to the club. It's surprising how many fall into the same category. Even people who handle death as part of their profession often find the subject awkward.

Doctors many times would rather run the other way than admit reality. Frequently they will ignore a patient rather than talk with him about the prospect of death.

A patient in the Midwest was dying from throat cancer and his deteriorating condition was obvious. Visitors remarked on his growing weakness. When cornered, the nurses would admit the hopelessness of the situation. But the report from the doctor remained unchanged: The patient is improving, the treatment is effective. Two weeks later the victim died. Those involved in the case have often wondered if that doctor's reports didn't indicate his inability to accept death. Doctors seem to be human also.

Sometimes ministers are no better equipped. One study of the dying suggests many pastors are as uncomfortable at the prospect of death as anyone else. They may try to get in and out of a hospital room as quickly as possible. Often they hide behind their Bibles and can hardly wait to read a verse, pray, and get out. Ministers seem to be human, too.

Dr. Elisabeth Kubler-Ross, authority on death and grief, offered noteworthy advice in a university lecture. She said she believes the greatest gift we can give our children is to have them around when a relative dies. It will help them face the reality of death and be better prepared for it.

One family turned a local tragedy into a learning experience for the children. A neighbor mother had been killed in an automobile accident, leaving two grade-school age children. Since both families were close, they became heavily involved in the funeral. Both families visited the funeral home to see the mother in her coffin. The children wanted to touch her and ask about her legs. To answer their curiosity the funeral director lifted the second section of the lid and showed her legs.

As they drove home the children were overflowing with questions. What happens when you die? Will the body stay like that? The son looked at his dad and asked, "If both of you get killed, what happens to me?"

It was a great opportunity to clear up questions. Their minds could be put somewhat at ease merely because they accepted the possibility of death.

A doctor who had watched many people die claims we have the wrong view. Where death is expected either through old age or an extended illness, he says, the process can be extremely peaceful. The scene is seldom characterized by the violent, dramatic trauma we may see in the movies. Certainly the few people I have seen die passed on with dignity, acceptance, and in some cases enthusiasm. The common ingredient among these was their willingness to discuss and face up to their own mortality.

If a couple is looking for a quiet, inexpensive, and romantic evening, they might try discussing death. It doesn't have to be a highly emotional, eruptive, or even sad affair. It can be deep, satisfying, and cementing. The two may find themselves more in love than they have been for some time. The episode will be a far cry from the superficial half-communication we experience most of the time.

One of the major concerns about modern funerals is the cost. They can be expensive or economical. Everyone suffers from rumors, fears, and a lack of information. Both the funeral industry and the public will be served by discovering the facts. Directors sometimes feel threatened and defensive. Families often feel intimidated and helpless. Healthy discussions will benefit both segments.

Make it a point to drive or walk through a cemetery. Visit a local mortuary. Spread out some literature and share ideas with your family. Then relax; you have handled one of the most important aspects of life.

TWO
THE CHRISTIAN
VIEW OF THE BODY

"Just feed me to the chickens." That was a popular saying when I was a child. People were trying to show their bravado at the thought of death. After all, no one is supposed to care what happens to his used body.

Today the same dark humor is still on parade. One night Johnny Carson, joking about his death, said he had the perfect plan. He merely wanted to be placed in a Hefty bag and deposited on the curb. The city could worry about disposing of him.

It was supposed to make people laugh, and it did. Even while I write the story down, I admit I am still amused by it.

But comedy and reality are sometimes worlds apart. What we say flippantly during one hour may not represent our values of a lifetime.

Whatever we say about funerals really pivots on our view of the importance of the body. What is its origin, its purpose, its future? These questions are the keys that unlock the subject.

In years of discussions about death, one guideline has become apparent. Usually little is accomplished by referring to our own bodies. When people must talk about their own death they often revert to a callous comedy approach. "Sprinkle my ashes over Cincinnati." A calmer perspective is possible by discussing a close loved one. What would you like to do with the body of your wife or child? That's not a pleasant thought, but it calls a person quickly back to reality. If a stable person wants his wife buried in a mass grave, or her body given to science, you know he is serious.

In seeking the Christian view of the body, our basic information source must be the Bible. Other sources can be helpful, but this one authority is primary. No one section or chapter of Scripture deals exhaustively with the subject, however. Rather, many passages convey an attitude, with plenty of examples.

The Bible avoids two popular approaches. It refuses to express either contempt or worship for the human body. Instead it maintains a consistent view which I refer to as *respect*. This simple principle can keep us from extremes in either direction.

To some, contempt for the human body seems like the pious route to travel. Proponents of this view hawk it as a solid act of faith. Since we believe in the eternal soul, they say, the remaining clay means nothing to Christians. But the contempt position lacks real support in Scripture.

We are expected to love our own bodies. (See Ephesians 5:28.) Any other attitude toward our bodies is an unhealthy distortion of our faith. At times, some have treated the flesh as the source of evil. "The sooner we can get rid of it, the better we can conquer sin." Religious fanatics of that persuasion have even tortured themselves, hoping by that to master the satanic influence.

But the Bible will not allow us to throw the blame on our bodies. If we live rebellious lives, we cannot escape responsibility for doing so. And to try to divide ourselves is simple dualism—a pagan practice which claims that I am one thing but my body is something else. Biblically, we are one with our bodies as long as our bodies are alive. And even our separation from them at death is only temporary; our spirits and our bodies will be reunited in the resurrection.

This is the reason why Paul wrote, "Do you not know that your bodies are members of Christ himself?" (1 Corinthians

6:15, NIV). Check the context of that verse and you see there's no ambiguity about the author's use of the word body. He is discussing the human, physical being. It's the apostle's basis for arguing against prostitution. A human body is a valuable gift from God—and *to* God. There is no room for contempt or dualism in this attitude.

Christian thought has its roots in Judaism. The Old Testament reports several famous instances in which particular care was taken to preserve a body. We don't need to labor the examples, but they are worth mentioning. For example, it says that the Lord buried Moses (Deuteronomy 34:6). We don't fully understand this statement, but we do see the careful attention of God being applied to a deceased body.

Look also at Joseph's attitude toward the dead body of his father Jacob. "Joseph threw himself upon his father's body and wept over him and kissed him" (Genesis 49:1, TLB). After forty days of embalming and seventy days of national mourning, Joseph transported his father's body back to Canaan. No quick quip like "Feed him to the chickens."

Later, before Joseph died, he asked to have his body returned to the homeland also. That was a way to express a reasonable love for a body which had served for a hundred years.

These examples do not necessarily argue for an elaborate or expensive funeral. But they do show a feeling far from contempt.

We are all familiar with the story of Christ's body on the cross. Joseph of Arimathea clearly risked his life to rescue the frame of the Son of Man. There would have been no point to such heroics if Christ's body was merely an expression of materialism. A body means something and must be treated with respect.

Whether our shell is cremated, buried, or donated, no matter whether we choose a $25 process or spend $5,000, the principle does not change. The body is a valued and loved vessel for which we have some great memories.

The other extreme we must reject is worship of the dead

21

body. That body may represent the real person, but it is not he. The components which make up the thinking and personality have now left. Soul, spirit, and mind are absent at death. "We are confident," wrote Paul, " . . . and would prefer to be away from the body and at home with the Lord" (2 Corinthians 5:8, NIV).

Here deep personal faith shows its strength. As Christians we believe the real person has left his body at death. Some groups do not hold this position. Their problems become more complicated. However, Paul and millions of Christians are convinced. And we attempt to carry out our faith in our funeral practices.

Some Christians then refuse to visit a cemetery. They feel it is morbid, especially since no one is actually "there." Others accept the grave site as a meaningful reminder. They have not forgotten and they will not. Either practice can fit within genuine Christian faith.

The person who has real problems is the one who maintains a morbid attachment to a grave site. Survivors who go to the cemetery for advice, or who seek to communicate with a dead loved one, have attributed too much strength to the corpse. Their preoccupation with the burial place indicates a personal problem. They may not be able to work out the reality of death. They need friendly, loving counsel.

Affection for the deceased body would be appropriate if we believed the soul was still housed in it. However, the Bible teaches us the exact opposite. Paul fully believed that at the moment he died he would go directly into the presence of God. (See 2 Corinthians 5:6, 7.) Then he would be at home in the place he had longed for ever since he had become a Christian.

The early Christians faced the same tensions on the subject as we do. During the second century (and some think the first), the believers had to find a way to bury their dead. Christians died or were slaughtered and their graves were not safe. Pagans hated them so strongly that they often hunted Christians even after death.

Believers were not content to abandon bodies. They had too

much respect. So they constructed underground cemeteries called catacombs. Bodies were buried there, and during persecution the Christians often conducted hidden worship services in the catacombs.

Those Christians had no contempt for the cadaver. They took enormous risks to secure a burial. However, their concern became overdone and they tripped over the second error. Soon the bodies of Christians came to be worshiped and their localities visited, in quest of devotional strength. The correct balance has always been difficult to hold.

The biblical concept of the resurrection of the body adds to our respect. The body is a valuable vessel but not an idol. Sometimes our problems are intensified because we imagine a body in heaven with an arm or kidney missing. Maybe we even picture it ashen or distorted in some other way. But those anxieties are unfounded. In heaven our bodies will be perfect regardless of their condition on earth.

How we understand the resurrection is at the core of funeral practices. It is easy to raise wild questions or to speculate endlessly. For instance, the question of the apple tree is suggested by antagonists and comedians. If an apple tree grows over a cemetery, how can there be a resurrection? After visitors eat the apples they may assimilate part of the deceased's body. Can God really separate all these particles at the resurrection?

If we donate our corneas, how will we see in the next life? Do we picture ourselves walking around eyeless? If we are cremated, will we be formless in eternity?

To some these questions are silly. To others they are serious or dormant in our consciousness. Until we grasp a biblical concept of resurrection, we are unlikely to become flexible.

It is easy to believe in a physical, factual resurrection of the human body. The Bible teaches it repeatedly. This resurrection will occur at a future day. There is no reason to think of the resurrected body merely as a spirit, or a feeling, or a vague renewal. The Christian's body will come back from the dead.

"So it will be with the resurrection of the dead. The body that is sown is perishable, it is raised imperishable; it is sown in dishonor, it is raised in glory; it is sown in weakness; it is raised in power; it is sown a natural body, it is raised a spiritual body" (1 Corinthians 15:42-44, NIV).

The fact of the resurrection has been a basic plank of the Christian faith. Yet the *form* of the resurrection is not nearly so clear. What will we look like? What will make up the new body? We have been notoriously unsuccessful in defining these. But maybe we are better off *admitting* we can't define everything, than taking wild shots in the dark.

We do know God will regather our body and bring it to heaven. It will be a changed body. It will be a reconstituted vessel. It would be foolish to limit God by our experience. A person may have had four kidney transplants. The last one worked. Now who will get which organ in eternity? This is a futile question which doesn't bother God at all.

From the human position God will have more difficult problems than this at the resurrection. However, locating parts or even cells may actually be no concern to him.

Paul's confidence is direct: "Our citizenship is in heaven. And we eagerly await a Savior from there, the Lord Jesus Christ, who, by the power that enables him to bring everything under his control, will transform our lowly bodies so that they will be like his glorious body" (Philippians 3:20-21, NIV).

Each body will be transformed by God's power. Somehow our vessel will be collected and changed. Whatever we do to ourselves will neither help nor hinder that transformation. God will recover decayed, burned, exploded, and "sawed asunder" bodies.

What will our bodies look like? Paul answered that precisely. They will be like Christ's "glorious body." It doesn't sound bad at all.

With this wholesome, healthy attitude toward the body, some guidelines are available for planning a funeral. The following suggestions are broad and will be discussed more fully later in this book.

The family should make considerable effort to carry out their personal preferences. A funeral can be conducted in any of a hundred different acceptable ways. Don't feel locked into any one pattern.

A funeral should depict an individual's taste, style, and Christian beliefs. Funeral practices are not eternal and were not dictated by Moses. The survivors must do what they feel is comfortable.

Whatever plans are made, they should not be an attempt to deny death. A hasty, impersonal disposal of the body may be deeply regretted later. So may an elaborate attempt to immortalize the person. Unfortunately, it's not uncommon for a family to try to rearrange a funeral months later.

The plans should include a respect for close friends and relatives. An aged mother may feel strongly about the burial of her adult daughter. A lifelong friend should not be ignored, because he hurts also. After the funeral the family will be glad they were considerate.

Careful thought should be given to the feelings of the deceased. If there is a certain funeral practice that the person especially disliked or one he particularly appreciated, these have to be considered. Funerals are for the living, but the living fare better knowing they have complied with the deceased's strong desires.

With these guidelines in mind, many variations are possible. A thorough discussion of them while we are in good health may result in a more satisfactory experience when the time comes.

The controversy about funerals has more twists than a dislocated snake. But one fact lifts its head above all the others. The surviving Christian must avoid trying to pay for his guilt by purchasing an elaborate funeral.

Few people will admit doing this, but the occurrence is not infrequent. A young husband feels he never gave his wife a good home during her life. Or he had a sexual affair which he kept secret. A wife nagged her husband and wants to say she is sorry.

All we know about sin and forgiveness tells us of the complete foolishness of trying to pay off our past. In the long run such a course of action only complicates the problem.

There is no doubt we are all guilty of mistreating the people we love. All of us could have been a little kinder. We all have said something thoughtless. Each of us could have kept a promise we chose to ignore. But no mistake can be resolved by lavish expenditure on a body. If anyone selects an expensive casket and a huge array of flowers, let it be for practically any reason other than to buy forgiveness.

The moment the person died the books closed on all we owed him. In a second that individual learned reams about the forgiveness of God. He no longer has reason to hold anything against you or me. Someday we will meet again in Jesus Christ and there will be only open acceptance and happiness (Revelation 21:3, 4).

If we care to, we are free to discuss our mistakes with God. The sincere confessor will find only forgiveness and reassurance. (See 1 John 1:8, 9.)

Nothing is more futile for the Christian than to seek absolution by spending. What could be more painful than to continue to carry the guilt?

THREE
BURIAL IN THE
BIBLE

The Bible contains few instructions concerning funerals. It devotes more attention to attitudes, inner peace, and eternity. Nevertheless, it becomes important to survey the practices in order to get a balanced outlook. We can see the concepts of respect and honest emotions expressing themselves in the Bible narratives.

Next to the tomb of Christ's burial, the most famous grave in the Bible is Machpelah. Evidently a family cave, Machpelah became the physical resting place for bodies of three generations of Abraham's family, including Sarah, Abraham, Isaac, Rebekah, Leah, Jacob, and possibly more.

Abraham bought the land when his wife Sarah died. It was owned by Ephron who sold it for 400 pieces of silver. The Canaanite offered to give it to the Hebrew, but Abraham insisted on paying.

Its location is given as a beautiful setting. The cave was at the end of a field and it was surrounded by trees (Genesis 23:17). Sarah had died at Hebron and was buried near Mamre. At the age of 127, Sarah had been through a great deal with her husband the Patriarch.

From what we know of ancient practices a sketchy outline of body preparation can be assumed. Sarah was probably not embalmed. Her body was wrapped in linen and packed with perfumes. A stone would have been rolled across the entrance to keep animals from attacking her cadaver. Later she was probably moved to one side of the cave to make room for other relatives.

The next one to join her was Abraham. There is no record of Abraham's other wives or concubines being buried at Machpelah. Abraham was 175 when he died (Genesis 25:9).

To appreciate how much this burial cave meant to the family, we need to weigh the death of Jacob. He died in distant Egypt under the protection of his son, Joseph. Realizing death was near, Jacob spelled out his funeral directions carefully.

Jacob wanted to be carried back to Canaan and buried at Machpelah. (The word *Machpelah* means double cave, indicating its size.) Jacob was not indifferent to the disposal of his body. At great work and expense, Jacob's remains were returned to the burial grounds of his fathers.

The Egyptians began to embalm Jacob's body at Joseph's command (Genesis 50:2). This was not a practice among the Jews. Normally they were buried immediately (Deuteronomy 21:22, 23). Both Jacob and his son Joseph were embalmed, but they were the rare exceptions.

The Jews seemed to have no intense dislike for embalming. At the same time they saw little use in it. They considered bodily decay to be the normal process. However, they did not take ground burial literally. Caves were their first preference. This was especially true in a small country which had little farmable land. The rocky ground which was more readily available was often unsuitable for burials.

Of the thousands of bodies which have been exhumed in Israel, practically none had been embalmed. The process, perfected by the Egyptians, was expensive and drawn out. Jacob's embalming took forty days. The normal procedure covered seventy days.

The embalmers removed the viscera and packed them in

jars. Usually the heart was left in the body. The cadaver was then packed in salt and spices. Other chemicals were also used. The body was then wrapped in linen.

Funeral directions left by the deceased were carried out to the letter. In the case of Jacob a long journey was necessary, but his wish was honored. If he had not been embalmed his children would probably still have delivered his bones to Machpelah.

Joseph died at the age of 110 and gave a request similar to his father's. He knew Israel would be freed from Egypt, and when they were, he wanted his body to be buried in the homeland. At death he was embalmed and placed in a coffin. There his remains waited for transportation to Canaan (Genesis 50:26).

Coffins were not normally used among the Jews. The ossuary box was common, but it contained only the bones after the body had decomposed.

A more frequent litter was the funeral bier. The was a wooden bed used to carry the body. It probably consisted of simple boards, though the wealthy may have had elaborately arranged ones.

David walked after the bier of Abner (2 Samuel 3:31). Jesus touched the bier during a funeral procession at Nain (Luke 7:14). Immediately the boy came back to life. The young lad sat up and talked to those standing around him.

What the Hebrews lacked in funeral ornaments they more than made up for in wailing and mourning. An expressive people, they cried loudly and beat on their own bodies. Often they would scream and tear their clothes. Over the centuries these customs changed only slightly.

Normally the mourning ceremony covered seven days. For some celebrities such as Moses and Aaron it continued for a month. Jacob's is probably the longest in the Bible, extending for seventy days.

They considered crying an important part of their release; professional mourners were often hired. These, paid for their services, resented anyone hurting their business. When Jesus raised a girl from the dead the singing mourners "scoffed and sneered" (Matthew 9:24).

Often poems and songs were written in honor of the deceased—much like today. When King Josiah was killed by an arrow, sad songs were written in his name. The songs were still sung by the population long after his death (2 Chronicles 35:25).

David, the famous king and psalmist, wrote several funeral poems. Saul, Jonathan, and Abner all were objects of his poetic mourning. When David recited his verse, the masses wept openly with their king. His funeral dirge was compiled into a book and read responsively by the people (2 Samuel 1:19ff).

Most Hebrew funerals were accompanied by musical instruments. The flute was the most popular because it could reach very high and very low notes. The Mishna insists on having instruments at even the most modest funerals. At services for the poor there were at least two flutes and one woman wailing.

The Jews did not care to reduce funeral services to the barest necessities. They looked for ways to vent their feelings—and they didn't like to do it alone.

As Judaism became more rigid and pharisaic, precise rules were developed to guide the family and its mourners. Barclay tells us these regulations centered on three areas.

The first concerned itself with the tearing of clothes. There are thirty-nine different guidelines to follow in this art. Enough garment had to be torn to expose some skin on the chest. The hole was to be left bare for the entire seven days. A woman was to tear her garment in private and then reverse it so as to protect her modesty.

The second area of mourning involved the professional wailers. When the prophet Jeremiah predicted destruction he told them (Jeremiah 9:17, 18) to call for mourners, who would then teach their daughters and neighbors to wail, because death would settle in.

Often mourners kept notes on the families they served. During their lamenting they would cry out the name of a sister, aunt, or uncle to show their personal touch. This way the procedure sounded almost natural.

Flute players made up the third segment of the ceremony. Other nationalities also placed heavy emphasis on this instrument because of its mournful sound.

While these were the general expressions of anguish, they were far from the only. Some would cover their faces or sprinkle ashes over their heads. Others would shave their heads, sit in silence, or fast. Often they would raise their hands into the air and cry out to God.

Two specific acts were condemned by the laws of Moses. Mourners were not allowed to cut themselves (Leviticus 19:28) or shave their eyelids or eyebrows (Deuteronomy 14:1). Both of these practices were considered pagan.

Neither Judaism nor Christianity accepted the process of cremation, though this form of body disposal was practiced by non-Christian Greeks and Romans. The rejection of cremation probably reflects on their beliefs about the resurrection. The Mishnah (early Rabbinic writings that shaped Jewish tradition) forbids cremation. And Constantine outlawed it for Christians in the fourth century.

What does this teach us by example? Probably not a great deal. Although cremation was rejected by the early Christians, there is no Scripture verse prohibiting it. Since the practice did exist, a law restricting its use was possible. Since the Bible is silent we are left to use our own intelligence.

A typical example of a first-century Jewish funeral is seen at the death of Lazarus (John 11). When he died his family buried him immediately in a cave or tomb. There his body would remain until it would decompose; then his bones would be put into an ossuary box. The box would be stored in the family cave.

Jesus did not come when he was first summoned, but he had reasons for waiting. Lazarus was a popular man and many friends journeyed to comfort the family. Bethany was only a couple of miles from Jerusalem, and many were able to make the trip.

When Christ arrived, Lazarus had been dead for four days. Yet the mourning continued. This was not unusual since it normally took a complete week (1 Samuel 31:13). When friends arrived even several days later, the wailing was profuse.

Lazarus' mourners behaved much like the comforters who had surrounded Job after his catastrophic losses (Job 2:13). Job's friends wailed for one week, tore their clothes, and threw ashes on their heads. Then they sat silently for a second week and sorrowed quietly.

The mourners who had packed Lazarus' house rose with Mary and followed her to Jesus and the tomb. Mary and her friends were weeping when they met Christ. Rather than discourage them he merely joined in by crying also. It was a natural expression for an outgoing people.

When the party arrived at the tomb, Jesus told them to remove the stone which blocked the entrance. It wasn't unusual for the stone to weigh a tone, requiring several men to move it.

Martha objected to opening the grave because Lazarus had been dead for four days. Unembalmed, he by now would have a "bad odor." But Jesus persisted and the stone was removed.

When Christ commanded him to come out, Lazarus staggered forward bound tightly in grave clothes. He was tied so tightly he probably could not have released himself from the wrappings in which perfumes were embedded to fight the stench.

The four-day period may be of special significance. Sometimes an individual was mistakenly buried alive. He might be up a day or even two days later. But it is highly unlikely that Lazarus had lived for *four* days in the tomb, only to arise at the sound of a voice. A miracle is the best explanation of this story.

After the crucifixion of Christ we again see the Jewish burial custom at work. Often the bodies of executed men were left for days on the cross, where they decayed and were mutilated by birds. Most of them would eventually be buried in a potter's field. Joseph of Arimathea and Nicodemus, at great risk to themselves, decided to give Jesus an honorable burial.

Both men may have been well off financially. At any rate they provided an expensive funeral for Jesus. They used 75 pounds of myrrh and aloes to prepare his body. They then took fine linen and wrapped the body carefully. The perfumes were mixed into the strips as they were stretched around him.

The rites were in keeping with ancient Jewish customs. When King Asa died, he was laid on a bed of perfume with sweet spices and ointments (2 Chronicles 16:14).

Near the place where Jesus was crucified there was a beautiful garden. Joseph had his personal tomb in that garden. He decided to bury Jesus there. It was not uncommon for wealthy people to have privately dug caves, used much as we use mausoleums today. Joseph's had never held a body before.

Joseph and Nicodemus did not take body disposal lightly. They accepted death but still held great respect for the body.

Some of the women followed Joseph and saw the tomb where Jesus was laid. They went home to gather more perfume, not because they considered the job done poorly; they merely wanted to add tokens of their love.

When Peter looked into the tomb he saw the linens lying unmoved. They were in the same position as when they wrapped Christ's body. He had left them without disturbing their shape.

The sole exception was the head napkin. This cloth had been folded neatly and left on the side by itself. The message was obvious. If someone had stolen the body he would not have taken time to undress it and neatly arrange the linen. If Christ had revived he would not have forsaken his clothing. The removal of the body was unusual. It was astounding. It was miraculous.

But how do biblical examples and practices apply to us? I believe they help us to keep our balance. Many of the practices which we label as pagan were actually used by the Hebrews and Christians. Some of them were originated by the early believers.

During the persecutions Christians took considerable pains to protect the bodies of believers. Rather than abandon them as useless or merely burn them, they took great risk to assure a proper burial. Beneath the city of Rome there are possibly 500 miles of catacombs in which Christians hid and buried their dead.

Many of these burial sites have a picture of a shepherd designed on the grave. The most popular artwork is that of the fish.

The basic ingredients in our present funeral practices are the same as those performed by first-century Hebrews and Christians. Mourning, the procession, the eulogy, funeral music, and the bier all find precedence during this era. While coffins and embalming are not common, neither are they condemned. Cremation was condemned by some Jewish officials but not directly by earliest Christianity.

Viewing of the deceased was practiced by the early Christians. Friends and relatives laid the body out, closed its eyes, and folded its hands. People would file past the corpse and have a final look. The burials were completed within eight hours or so. The heat and rejection of embalming would not allow a longer viewing.

The Hebrews firmly condemned the parting kiss on the deceased. However, early Christianity did not. The Christian "kiss of peace" constituted a serious departure from Jewish practice. Some Christians still do this soon after a person dies.

The practice of straightening out the legs probably has a superstitious origin, though used by Christians. Some felt the soul could leave smoothly through the mouth if it did not have to curve through the body. Other cultures return their dead to a prenatal position.

Early Christians soon found marked differences in their practices from Hebrew traditions. Time and the assimilation of non-Jewish converts made these changes easier. Instead of

practicing the ancient wailing, Christians became more sub-
dued and calm. Many considered it a more fitting testimony to
their trust in God.

Christians began the "wake" or "watch." Someone stayed
with the body for the entire eight hours before its burial. They
seemed to have a dual motive. It didn't seem polite to leave the
corpse alone, and someone should be there in case it regained
consciousness—not a likely prospect, but not impossible
either.

The funeral procession soon lost its open wailing. Christian
leaders felt it was unfitting for believers to act in such a manner. Noisy displays of grief were frowned on.

Young men volunteered to carry the bier to the grave site.
The procession usually consisted of the corpse, the bearers, the
family, and friends. Flowers were often scattered on the grave
site.

When the church gained its liberty in the fourth century, its
funeral practices changed. Cemeteries above the ground became popular again. The funeral service soon moved into
the church, where it remained for many centuries.

Problems with funerals set in early after the Christians
acquired their liberty. At first believers prepared bodies for
each other, thus avoiding the costly assistance associated with
paganism. But before long they assimilated the same system
and its costs.

Poor people felt oppressed under the new financial arrangements and organized burial clubs. Constantine tried to offset
the worsening practice by guaranteeing everyone a decent
burial. Each church was told to provide a coffin, a cross bearer,
eight monks, and three acolytes for any Christian burial.

The church appointed the first funeral directors, who were
similar to those who worked at that trade in Rome. They
cared for the entire service, including grave-digging, preparation of a coffin, and other functions.

FOUR
VIEWING THE BODY

"I want the funeral done as cheaply as possible. And I certainly don't want the body embalmed." He had sold real estate for years and was trying to be practical about death. Naturally the second question had to be asked.

"What about your wife? How do you picture *her* funeral?"

"Well, that might be different. In her day she was a beautiful woman. I think people should get to say goodbye to her. And of course we would want to allow time for her sister to get here from the coast."

This ambivalence is typical of many people. We have a desire to pare down a funeral to the bare necessities. At the same time we want to use conveniences.

One of the most unsettling areas surrounding funerals is the question of embalming. Is this process really necessary? To some of us it sounds ghoulish and pagan. Possibly it is an unnecessary expense we would be better off without.

In most localities a body does not have to be embalmed. This comes as a surprise to great numbers of people. During this century we have routinely preserved bodies. But Americans haven't always. Generally we embalm because of choice and custom rather than because of rock-bottom necessity.

There are three good reasons to embalm a body. (1)

Embalming is necessary if a body is to be transported on a common carrier taking several hours or days. (2) If certain infectious diseases caused death, embalming may be a necessary safeguard. (3) Embalming makes public viewing more acceptable.

Normally the law is concerned with only the first two problems. However, most of Western population seems intent on the third.

The desire to keep a body for three or four days before burial is as old as America. Soon after families arrived in the colonies they began to spread out. Brothers, sisters, children moved twenty, forty, a hundred miles away. But when someone died the relatives tried to gather for the funeral. Because travel took time, some preservation was essential.

During the winter it was easier to keep a body. Cold weather retarded the decaying process. In the summer perfumes held the odor in check to a degree, but the battle wasn't easy.

Distance was only one of the difficulties. Sometimes a poor family couldn't afford a coffin or a burial plot. Often the merchant would merely hold the body until money could be raised.

The science of embalming had largely been abandoned for 1,500 years. In some cases bodies were preserved in vats of alcohol. One young woman's body was kept this way because her family didn't want to bury her at sea. Several famous leaders' bodies were preserved, but only at considerable expense and labor.

During the 1700s funerals became more open and popular in this country. Elaborate sermons were delivered at funerals, and often copies of the sermons were distributed afterward, in pamphlets bordered in black, with a skull and crossbones at the top. After-funeral drinking festivals and banquets became both popular and expensive. In some areas laws were passed to curb the excesses.

In the current of change the population saw more need to prepare a body to be kept presentable for several days. As the demand increased the methods naturally were improved.

Experiments in arterial and cavity embalming were carried on by pioneers such as William Hunter. Abuses arose to give the process a bad name. Martin Van Butchell had his wife embalmed and kept her in the living room for months. Encased in glass, she was seen by visitors each day from nine to one, excluding Sundays. When Van Butchell remarried, his new wife insisted on shipping her predecessor to a local museum.

The Civil War brought embalming into modern prominence. There was a cry to have fallen officers returned to their home states. President Lincoln and his son Willie were embalmed by injection.

To properly evaulate the significance of embalming, certain historical realities have to be weighed. The process is not eternal. Countless millions have been buried without it. Even in the United States and Canada, large numbers still are.

A second consideration is the demand for embalming. The funeral business did not invent embalming and push it on the American people. The populace asked for it as times changed. The fact that most of us still select it seems to indicate a sense of need for it to this day.

At the turn of the present century embalming was a highly controversial subject. More bodies were buried without than with arterial embalming. Both Christians and humanitarians often objected strenuously. They had visions of bodies being severely mutilated. Ministers denounced it as a desecration of "the temple of God."

We often discuss this subject with one eye closed. If we do not want or need it, the practice could die immediately. But the individual decision must be made after considering the facts. It would be mindless either to blindly accept or to blindly denounce the practice.

This is one of the reasons why this book will outline the process itself. Both the public and the funeral business suffer because of widespread ignorance on the subject.

The basic questions are: Do we want to preserve the body? Why? How long?

Begin with the last question. How long do you want to

preserve a body? Three days, a week, ten years, forever? With the fluids presently available, a body can be kept intact for decades and beyond. The skin will become leathery, but the basic features will remain. If extra chemicals are added, some discoloring may appear, but the body will be preserved longer.

Fortunately, most people are not interested in extended periods. Some who are, might benefit from solid counseling toward accepting death. Benjamin Franklin, and a few current groups, had hopes of eventually reviving bodies after a century of death. But not many share the prospect.

If, however, we want to keep the body for several days, the embalming process is ideal. It protects the corpse until the family can gather.

Embalming is not the ghoulish mutilation many people fear. The public needs to know more about the subject. Ignorance is often the enemy of the funeral director.

Normally the process consists of one incision. It is often made at the groin but can be near the ankle or at the lower neck. Preserving fluids are sent into the system while the blood is drained. The liquid replacement is done efficiently and neatly.

In most cases a second step is necessary to prevent disfigurement. Internal organs are likely to gain gas and bloat the body. Consequently, abdominal organs are punctured. Otherwise it would be risky to display the body.

To make the face presentable several steps may be taken. Materials are placed under the eyelids to prevent them from opening. If this precaution is not taken, the lids may have a tendency to slide up slightly. The jaws are then fastened together to keep the lower jaw from dropping.

Methods differ with community and practitioner, but basically these are the essential steps. Without them most people would not care for a viewing which lasts three or four days. Consequently, the funeral director provides an essential service for any family that wants an open casket.

Cosmetology is the final preparation. This could include a permanent or a haircut. Then makeup is applied. Funeral directors have training in this art. To some extent they can make restorations on a face that has been damaged.

In most cases the family supplies clothing for the body. If suitable clothing is not available the director can provide a selection.

Funeral directors normally have a balanced attitude. There is a respect for the body. No unnecessary changes are made. At the same time they accept the absence of life. The person is dead. They do not hesitate to perform essential functions.

When a member of our family dies we are not in a position to perform these duties. Two centuries ago our neighbors or friends may have carried them out. As society changed, we turned more to professionals. This has been the trend in many fields. Soon we sought individuals to "undertake" these jobs at death. They became the "undertakers."

The funeral director provides the few functions which are essential. In addition he offers many services we want. The majority of us seem to want a viewing. The funeral director makes this possible. If the American public rises up and says, "We don't want it anymore," the director will stop doing it. The entire process is as simple as supply and demand.

It is true that not all directors explain the options. Our personal responsibility is to discover the open avenues and discuss them. Possibly we will choose to keep our current practice, or maybe not. But at no point can we blame the funeral director for our refusal to face reality and make decisions.

One aspect of modern funerals which has to be discussed is the practice of open coffins. Is it necessary to see a body in order to complete the grief process? Or is this a hoax promoted by special interest groups?

A decade ago two men drowned in suburban Detroit. Their bodies were trapped under the ice and recovery was impossible. The families had to wait until spring before a funeral could be conducted. The time span was one of pure agony. Certainly these families were unable to work out their grief for months.

But under average circumstances, is a viewing essential? The funeral industry contends that it is. Occasionally they will publish the opinion of a psychologist who contends that an open casket completes the grief process. Raether and Slater represent this position:

"Man makes meaningful associations with persons and significant objects. When someone dies, a life on earth has ended. What remains is not that living person, it is the body of a man, woman or child who once was loved and who loved in return. When we remember a person we have known, we always think of them in terms of their physical being—their body.

"That is why it is difficult for many survivors to disassociate themselves immediately from the lifeless body. The finite mind requires evidence that an earthly existence has ended. With the body present, the opportunity is thus provided for recall or reminiscence, both of which help in accepting the reality and finality of the death that has occurred" (*Concerning Death*, p. 194).

Those who recommend viewing as a psychological necessity do it on several grounds. They believe mobile families are one reason. Since relatives are often away at the time of death, an open casket is the chance to say goodbye. Large numbers of people die in hospitals or elsewhere away from home. A viewing may be a way to call everything together again, offering a reflective pause in the fast-moving tragedies of life.

A viewing may also help friends and relatives to accept the reality of a loved one's death. When the fact of a death is not permitted to soak in and be adequately realized, alarming consequences could result later.

A husband in Spokane tried to arrange a highly efficient funeral for his wife. He wanted the service carried out quickly. The coffin was a cheap model and without vault. The viewing time was kept to a minimum. He considered this the sensible way to accept death. One week later he returned to the funeral director greatly disturbed. Unable to sleep, he wanted to "redo" the funeral. Was there some way to re-bury his lovely wife? he wondered. When shortcuts are taken to deny the reality of death, the aftereffects can be devastating. We will be wise not to rush into a choice of arrangements that we might regret.

Those who argue for a viewing stress the importance of peaceful recall. Many die after lingering and disfiguring illnesses. Others are violently killed in auto accidents. Funeral directors can usually do an excellent job of restoration. This allows the survivors to have a last look or "memory picture." This experience can often be therapeutic. Children may be the main benefactors of a peaceful "farewell."

A lady in the Chicago area experienced an "efficient" funeral for both her parents. It was their choosing, and she complied. However, she looks back on the service as hollow and unfulfilling. For her it was an emotional disaster. She wanted to bid farewell to each of her parents but they weren't there. Their bodies had been disposed of immediately after death. She begs the rest of her relatives to skip the "supermarket" approach.

Rabbi Steven Jacobs argues passionately for the viewing and traditional service. He feels strongly that we know everything in life by our senses. We need to see, feel, and even touch to be reassured of the reality of death.

In his ministry Rabbi Jacobs sees an increasing number of cremations. He doesn't object. His only complaint is the "assembly line" approach that some crematories use. Merely trying to get rid of the body as quickly as possible seems to have no particular merit. He wants a place: a grave, a niche, where death has definitely been finalized.

Pastor Bob Brown of Trinity Baptist Church in Lexington, Kentucky, feels the same way. He calls the viewing of a lifeless corpse the most dramatic and positive way to face the reality of death. He believes one of the real values of the public funeral is its ability to soften the experience of bereavement. It allows the person to leave our life more slowly and with some gentleness.

Pastor Brown's views, appearing in the *Church Herald*, drove home one particular point which should not be missed. We would be foolish to base funeral plans on hostility toward funeral directors. Some people are determined that directors are crooks and that they will not be allowed to make money out of this death. Individuals who feel this way need some kind of counseling. Whatever their choices in funeral practice, they cannot be decided satisfactorily on this level.

Those who feel strongly about the public viewing of bodies often list three therapeutic purposes. One is realization. Seeing the dead body helps solidify the fact in our minds. A second purpose is recall. It provides us with an opportunity to take a final mental picture and hold it. The body doesn't look alive and really shouldn't, but many feel the restored look is so much better than the image of suffering which otherwise might be predominant. The third reason is an opportunity for expression. It gives the friends and relatives a focal point. They can meet, express their love for the person, and let their feelings out. The occasion releases some of the tension and grief.

Naturally many people do not agree with this assessment. Some even feel it is purely a ploy of the funeral industry to keep their business going and prosperous. The dissenters do have a point. Not everyone needs our typical viewing or traditional funeral. But many others do, and this is why the options must be available.

The Wilbert Vault Company asks penetrating questions in the survey they commissioned on funeral attitudes. Only 7½ percent said they did not want a funeral with friends and relatives present when a relative died. This affirms that 92½ percent of Americans want some sort of get-together on that occasion.

Only 15 percent considered funerals burdensome and unnecessary. However, another 15 percent remained undecided. These figures suggest considerable flexibility and ambivalence. Possibly the most telling statistic on this aspect of funerals concerns our adjustment at the death of a loved one. Forty percent were not sure that funeral services really helped in this area.

I conclude therefore that the viewing of the body is a decided help to most relatives, though it is not necessary for everyone.

It goes back again to individual preferences. Ideally each of us will face these decisions and make them as they best suit us and our situation.

If you are interested in more information from the industry's perspective you could write the National Funeral Directors Association, 135 West Wells Street, Milwaukee, WI 53203, or the National Funeral Directors and Morticians Association, 734 West 79th Street, Chicago, IL 60620.

FIVE
COSTS, CASKETS, AND HEADSTONES

For most Americans a funeral is the third largest purchase they will ever make. Normally only homes and automobiles cost more. This may be money well spent, but it should not be accepted lightly.

As of this writing, the average person pays $2,000 from the time the funeral director is contacted until the grave is closed. For some people it represents a reasonable expenditure with little or no inconvenience. To others it becomes an unreasonable burden and should be reduced.

Before we can delve deeply into this question, certain guidelines must be established. The first one is that it is unfair to expect funeral directors to operate without a profit. Grocers give practically no food away. The local furniture store has given me no free chairs. Services and merchandise cost money. Most of us need funeral directors and appreciate them. They must make a profit.

The second guideline is to stop trying to pay for our sins. In a checkbook society we are practicing checkbook redemption. We often act as if we are attempting to clean our slate by buying an elaborate funeral. We didn't visit grandmother at home but we will try to make it right now. Someone's career kept him from spending time with his wife so an expensive casket is "the least I can do."

There is a vast difference between showing love and buying forgiveness. The Bible is relentless at this point. Forgiveness can be neither earned nor purchased. It says, rather: "Be gentle and ready to forgive; never hold grudges. Remember, the Lord forgave you, so you must forgive others." (Colossians 3:13, NIV).

A funeral can be therapeutic when it is part of an expression of love. It may be pagan if it is a search for forgiveness.

The third significant guideline is the need to face up to our mortality. We are going to die. Unless Christ returns during our lifetime, we will complete the normal process of life. We need to make decisions and even do some comparative shopping.

When we purchase a car we might visit half a dozen dealers. However, when someone dies we do not have time to compare. Consequently, we pay whatever we must. But those who are unhappy with funeral costs must be willing to shop and ask questions. Most of us are people of moderation. We probably wouldn't select the cheapest funeral and neither would we pick an extravagant one. The moderate average funeral will suit most of us fine.

But what are we talking about? In Washington, D.C., there are fifty-five funeral homes. If a local resident called around and asked for prices, he would find a wide range. Funeral homes differ on their "average" funeral as much as $1,300 from one mortuary to the next. Yet they provide basically the same funeral. If you ask them for the least expensive service they have, the difference between lowest and highest minimum is more than $700.

If our first consideration is economy the individual must comparison-shop ahead of time. Otherwise time restricts him to the prices available in one or two local mortuaries.

From the number of complaints registered, we must conclude that most people are reasonably content with the funeral prices they pay. Mind you—not necessarily happy, because spending discourages most of us. But for those who are looking to reduce the cost, comparison shopping and early decision making are their best allies.

If an individual is seeking the least expensive funeral, he may choose immediate cremation. A survey of the mortuaries in Washington, D.C., brought a similar result. The price can double from one business to the next.

For many families, cost is not the deciding factor. They have met and dealt with a funeral director, and are pleased with his way of relating to them. They realize they may be able to beat the price somewhere else but that doesn't excite them. Familiarity and trust are important and should not be ignored. This is the same reason for buying a refrigerator from someone we know. If it costs a little more it may be worth it.

Others appreciate the location of a particular mortuary. To shop around may mean leaving the neighborhood or even the town. For a couple of hundred dollars difference they would rather stay close.

Those with religious or ethnic preferences are often happy to pay extra. They feel more at home in familiar surroundings. One funeral home will get a large percentage of Lutheran funerals or a considerable number of Catholic.

Another segment of society tries to combine the best elements of both. They have already selected a funeral home but now need to determine a price range. Before death visits their family, they have visited the funeral home and made important decisions. The individual has chosen the type of casket and considered the pros and cons of a vault.

Dry eyes and a happy heart are most likely the best atmosphere for making funeral decisions. Some call on their minister and share ideas about the service and various practices. Some discuss the relative merits of cremation.

Generally, funeral directors recognize the benefits of early shopping and will welcome a visitor. They want satisfied customers. A thoughtful purchase leaves everyone with fewer regrets.

Some who try to make plans early also go as far as paying for their funeral in advance. There are advantages, since the purchaser then knows the arrangements are definite.

There are several drawbacks to paying cash in advance. The most obvious is the possibility you may move. When you leave the area it could be difficult to get your money back as quickly and smoothly as you might like.

Another disadvantage is the sharp change which could occur in cost. If prices rise or fall drastically, the deposit could be affected accordingly. Some contracts contain clauses which release the director from furnishing a funeral at the set price. Nevertheless it might be something you will want to discuss with your director.

A funeral director will help us arrive at a financial range if we want him to. Most people have a Social Security benefit of over $250 coming, if they have paid into the system. The Veteran's Administration could pay another $250. They may also furnish a cemetery plot and headstone. Some people have labor union or fraternal benefits coming. A mortician can help make these contacts.

The first area to consider is whether or not you want a fairly traditional funeral. Most of us do. But if you want any deviations such as immediate disposition or no embalming, now is the time to discuss them. Don't be afraid to ask about anything which interests you. A good funeral director will be open and willing to discuss. If he isn't, you will know you are in the wrong establishment. Generally directors accept you as the customer and will make a reasonable attempt to please.

At this point ask to see his price list. How much are his services currently? You realize that five or ten years from now they will be different. Ask if you have to purchase the entire package or if you can subtract or change a few items. Some directors will allow alterations and others will not. If this is important to you, it may be necessary to shop around.

In many funeral homes the price of a service is exactly the same for everyone. The important difference in that particular home is the cost of the casket. Ask the director to show you the caskets and explain the price ranges.

A gentleman in suburban Detroit did this in a satisfying way. He wasn't trying to get the cheapest coffin possible or strike a deal. Death might not come for thirty years. But he did want to give a preference on the type of casket and vault. This removed the pressure from his survivors. They would not have to spend agonizing time trying to guess what he "would have wanted." They know. He told them.

Most funeral homes seem to display more middle- and higher-priced caskets than inexpensive ones. However they do want your business and will make lower-priced ones available if you persist. They are in the service of providing funerals. They are also in the business of selling caskets. Naturally they hope to sell the best casket they can. People in other businesses do the same thing.

The key to a funeral director's financial success is the casket. If he does not make it here, under the present setup his business will hurt. Consequently, he will give greater prominence to his better models. When a customer purchases a high-priced casket, the director's heart has to skip a happy beat.

The fact also remains that if most people buy the cheaper models he will be forced to carry more of them. The economy-conscious consumer must learn to push for the less expensive casket. The funeral director will continue to make the better models more obvious for the sake of profits.

Wooden caskets can be less expensive than the metal, but not necessarily. Don't merely enter a funeral home determined to get wood and save.

A few funeral directors are aggressive in trying to point to the more expensive models. One family in Delaware reports a terribly dissatisfying experience. They had dealt with the funeral home before so they were particularly shocked. In this instance the director kept pushing toward the more expensive models. The family, in a poor mood to resist, felt they were being taken advantage of.

Generally funeral directors are too wise for this. It is quite common to have a mortician accompany the family into the display room, show the range of selections, answer questions, and then politely leave. The family is free to discuss the relative merits of the caskets and make the decision. Many directors are sensitive to criticism and will go out of their way to be gentle, open, and soft-sell in this area.

One thing is certain. Funeral directors will not carry caskets which people do not want. They can't afford such extravagance. In Washington, D.C., one-third of the funeral homes have no display room at all because their overhead is so costly. If we resist caskets with special mattresses and cranking headlifts, naturally they will stop carrying them. In the same vein, if we keep asking for the less expensive caskets, they will have to carry more of them.

We can't expect the director to push the inexpensive funeral. But if those are our choices, he will conform.

After discussing the coffin, take time to gather information on vaults and concrete containers. Many people want them. Their basic purpose is to prevent water from getting into the casket (only the vault does this). Their other function is to keep the ground from caving in if the casket collapses.

There is a tremendous amount of ignorance concerning burial vaults. The results of the Wilbert survey show that only 15 percent of the population felt they had a good understanding of the purpose of a vault. Consequently, education is important. Some will purchase a vault when they don't really want one. Others will buy a container and later wonder why. It is better to discuss it intelligently and have a basis for the decision.

A vault is a metal or concrete box which is placed first into the grave to hold the casket. After the casket has been placed in it, the vault is sealed shut to hold out water and to protect against a cave-in. Some cemeteries demand them.

Caskets providing both of these features can be purchased. Metal caskets are available which will not leak and are too strong to crush under normal circumstances.

Paramount to this question is our feeling toward natural decomposition. Is it really important to preserve the body?

Are we content to let its components break down and return to nature? In most cases there was no such interest in the Bible. Maybe we have become too preoccupied with this vague desire to preserve a body.

The concrete container does not resist water but will help prevent cave-in. At this writing, those who purchase containers are choosing the concrete variety three times as often as vaults.

Caskets and vaults can both be avoided if the individual chooses cremation. A few funeral homes eliminate the casket even if there is a cremation with a viewing. In most states a casket is not required for a cremation. It is important to know this because some directors will not volunteer this information. A few don't even know it themselves. Generally a cremation without a viewing does not need a casket. Push for information on alternatives if you want them.

The next major decision which must be faced is the cemetery. The choices are wide and the regulations and costs may vary considerably. There are 9,000 active cemeteries in the United States, and of these 3,000 are privately owned and operated. The other 6,000 are owned by nonprofit groups or municipalities. Usually the public-owned cemeteries are less expensive. There are 103 national cemeteries and about half of them have openings for those who are eligible.

Before deciding on a cemetery be sure you understand their rules and regulations. Some will allow monuments, others won't. One will demand a vault and the next one doesn't care. Here again it pays to shop around and ask questions. Be sure the cemetery you have in mind suits your taste and pocketbook. The initial cost of the plot plus opening and closing the grave may be six times as high in one cemetery as the next. Yet they may offer the exact same service.

A cemetery's rules may escalate the cost fantastically. The cemetery which both demands a vault and also sells vaults may not always have the customer's best interest at heart. Those who insist the consumer buy the marker from them should be treated with caution.

It may be a wise move to visit a few cemeteries and make comparisons. Many will want to purchase their plot early to avoid the pressure later.

The final purchase will concern monuments and markers. Prices and taste differ immensely. When you visit a cemetery it is easy to see why so many people buy markers. Part of it stems from respect and love. Another part must certainly come from social pressure. It would be difficult to leave your relative without a headstone when so many others have them.

Monuments are not cheap and should be purchased with care. Be sure that any you select carries a "double protection." This means that either the purchaser or the cemetery can make a claim for repair or replacement free of charge.

The best quality stone is granite. It is the most durable monument. Granite is available in half a dozen colors. If it is good quality it will be flawless and hold a true color. Marble, slate, and sandstone do not hold up as well. Sandblasting and polishing are painstaking jobs and naturally make the product expensive. Some granite monuments have remained undamaged for thousands of years.

The amount of work involved, the size, and the quality of stone, each may alter the cost considerably. And the same monument could cost twice as much from one dealer to another. It is easy to spend a few hundred dollars or a few thousand.

Cemeteries often have restrictions on the type of memorial stones which can be used. While you are checking them out make sure the cemetery agrees with your plans for a monument.

Memorial parks will allow only flat markers of granite, bronze, or both. These markers are usually a good deal cheaper. Maintenance costs are lower in memorial parks.

If you have chosen cremation, all of the above options are open plus a few more. An urn could be purchased to hold the remains—but it is not necessary. A burial plot could be purchased, a niche in a columbarium could hold the remains, or else the ashes can be returned to the family. Do not let directors tell you that the remains cannot be given to you personally. In most cases they can.

When a family is eligible for veteran's benefits, the Veterans Administration makes a headstone or grave marker available at no cost. They also supply free transportation of the marker to the cemetery of your choice. A private cemetery will probably charge to install it.

In some areas "picture" monuments are becoming popular. A photograph of the individual is mounted onto the stone and covered with a clear shield. Often the pictures are in color and some of them are old photographs.

There will be more expenses than we have mentioned here. Most of them will be small. You will need to pay for death certificates and possibly a fee for an organist, a singer, a clergyman, flowers, and other "extras" which can total a few hundred dollars. These may not be indicated in the initial estimate of the cost of the funeral.

Prices will mean little to a certain segment of our population. They may have considerable financial resources or a healthy insurance policy. Their first concern is doing everything the way they want it, and cost is secondary. This is their privilege.

There is another portion of the population which has adequate funds but considers an expensive funeral a waste. They would rather divert their money to what they see as more worthy causes. Body disposition does not seem worthy of a sizable expenditure. Some even look on it as pagan.

A third group exists which is in fact hard pressed. It is not a question of what they would like to do but what they must do. It is unwise for them to go into deep debt to purchase ornate trappings for a funeral.

Whatever our feelings, our options are there for the claiming. Those who have the freest choices are those who comparison shop before the death occurs.

Every year more widows are left than widowers. Presently women are losing husbands at five times the rate of men losing wives. This gives us a good picture of who is usually being left to make funeral arrangements. Most often it is a bereaved woman surrounded by relatives and friends. She could be helped considerably if we make some wise decisions for her.

If you would like more information on cemeteries or monuments, visit your local directors or dealers, or write any of the following: American Cemetery Association, 250 East Broad Street, Columbus, OH 43215; American Monument Association, 6902 North High Street, Worthington, OH 43085; Monument Builders of North America, 1612 Central Street, Evanston, IL 60201; or National Association of Cemeteries, 1911 North Ft. Meyers Drive, Arlington, VA 22209.

SIX
THE CREMATION
QUESTION

"Burning the body of someone you love sounds like a horrible thing to do."

"But cremation is such a clean, efficient way to dispose of a body which otherwise only decays."

These two opinions seem to pair off the most popular positions on cremation. More people are starting to consider it. Is it better than a shrine in the ground? Is it less expensive? What happens to the ashes? Is cremation a legitimate Christian practice, or is it a pagan ritual or a communist plot?

Attitudes toward cremation are changing. A hundred years ago the church, synagogue, and many other segments of society fought it like a mother protecting her cubs. Today the practice is growing steadily in several countries and stampeding in others.

In Japan 75 percent are choosing cremation. The British have passed the 60 percent mark, while Australia and New Zealand hover at 30 percent. In recent years crematories have seen a noticeable increase of business in the United States, with more than 140,000 cremations performed here annually.

The popularity of cremation is growing steadily if not rapidly. In 1974 6.18 percent of all American funerals included cremation. The next year it rose to 6.55 percent. By 1976 the statistics had pushed to 7.32 percent. How sharply these figures will rise in the future is uncertain. Most of the two million annual funerals are still patterned after the traditional form. A considerable percentage of those choosing cremation prefer a viewing, flowers, and an expensive casket to go with it.

The practice has come a long way since Henry Thompson organized the Cremation Society of England in 1874. His book, *Cremation: The Treatment of the Body after Death,* insulted a lot of consciences. It took him four years to gain permission to build a crematory. Thirty years later a Cremation Act was passed.

World War 2 made the biggest change in England's attitudes concerning cremation, because the government then recognized its critical space problem and began to promote cremation.

In the early days cremation was less refined, though effective. F. J. LeMoyne built the first crematory in America, at Washington, Pennsylvania. His 1876 model was a simple furnace.

In our modern setting, more than 230 crematories dot the land. However, rumors pester the business like mosquitoes at a cookout. No aspect is more muddled for the public than the question of cost.

A man called his local funeral home. His elderly aunt had died. She had little in life, and the responsibility for her funeral fell to his shoulders. He asked his respected funeral director for a nice, low-cost cremation.

The mortician told him the simple facts. The cost of a full-service cremation is often *higher* than other funerals. That doesn't sound right. How much could it cost to incinerate a corpse?

One decision determines the expense more than any other. Does the family want a viewing? If they do, the cost remains on the same level as a traditional burial service.

It is true that cremation can be inexpensive if performed in three simple steps. The funeral director can pick up the body at the hospital and deliver it to the crematory where the body is promptly reduced to "cremains." The ashes are then presented to the family for disposal.

This type of cremation is about as basic as the process can get. It isn't absurd for a family to do this. If they choose to, they may conduct a memorial service later. The total cost of this operation runs in the area of a few hundred dollars. Some people select this inexpensive funeral process. They have decided on a nonviewing service.

However, a cremation with a viewable body reintroduces the serious cost factor. A sincere businessman was intent on escaping the "senseless" expense and "foolish" funeral practices. But of course, he did not want to bury his wife until his children arrived from the East Coast. The decision to wait and have a viewing brought him back into the conventional form.

The four steps which escalate the funeral expenses are: embalming, cosmetizing, casket, and use of the chapel. These are essential to most viewings.

For instance, a family can select an inexpensive container for a cremation. Yet they are less likely to make this choice if friends and relatives are going to line up and see it.

Caskets can range in cost from several hundred dollars to a rare $20,000. Many come complete with a spring mattress for "the latest in comfort." If the family chooses, the cremation, too, can be a very expensive process. *Changing Times* magazine in 1976 reported the following costs by crematories. The actual cremation itself could cost from $50 to $300. A bronze urn to hold the ashes or cremains can run from $100 to $250. Many people select a niche to hold the remains. This is a burial place in a columbarium or concrete building. The listed price of a niche ranges from $75 to $750. By this time the cost has doubtless risen. These charges will be on top of the funeral director's costs.

It is safe to say that the cost factor cannot be the primary motivation for choosing cremation. The question of a viewing must be settled first. The best time to discuss these options is while we are healthy and able to make calm choices.

As odd as a nonviewing sounds, it is common. In many countries it is a predominant practice.

Aside from the question of cost, what really happens during a cremation? Is it a process we want to use in disposing of bodies?

Many who select cremation see it as a quick, clean reduction of the body. They prefer it to a slow process in the ground or in a tomb. They sometimes see embalming as an attempt to resist this natural process.

A funeral director will deliver the body to a crematory. In most areas the presence of a mortician is required by law. The purpose is to help discourage any criminal elements who might want to dispose of a body without questions.

The body must be in a suitable container. In different states the required type of receptacle will differ. An expensive casket is not necessary. The casket will be heated with the body in it. Afterwards the container will be destroyed if it did not burn.

Two methods are used in cremation. Some organizations use direct fire. Others use only heat supplied electrically. This second process is called calcination. In two to three hours the body is reduced to elementary pieces of bone. These leftover parts are then placed into an urn or container of the family's choice. The remains can be mailed if they are to be delivered to a distant place.

If cremains are to be scattered, another process is necessary. The remaining bones have to be pulverized. The local crematory can take care of this. Some crematories discourage scattering. Listen to them carefully but cautiously. They also sell urns, niches, and often cemetery lots. These business interests could indicate an acute case of bias.

The family may want to select the storage facilities offered by the crematory. But scattering is a valid choice. In most states the practice, called "strewing," is perfectly legal and acceptable. In England most cremains are strewn.

A crematory may even offer a special garden where remains are regularly distributed. Some families choose to plant a tree or a bush as a living memorial. The options are broad. Don't let anyone talk you into doing something you do not really care to.

People select cremation for a variety of reasons. In some cases the motivation is regrettable. Probably the greatest reason in many countries is the acute problem of space. Certainly both England and Japan are facing this crisis. The United States may or may not be staring down this barrel. In metropolitan areas the scarcity of land is a pressing issue. However, in many areas the cemetery business is highly lucrative and there is little danger of its annihilation.

The Woodlawn Cemetery in the Bronx of New York believes cremations will increase sharply in the next twenty years. According to their calculations there are only 190 acres of empty cemetery lots left in the five boroughs of New York City. Given the present rate of burials, some drastic change will be necessary. In response to this trend the cemetery has constructed a new crematory. They expect 3,000 cremations annually in this facility alone. They see the emphasis on cremation as a fight for business survival. The only way to stay in business is to accommodate themselves to what they feel will be the obvious trend. There are already four other crematories in the area, but they feel there will be no infringement.

A second reason is personal preference. The family chooses a speedy reduction of the body. This is a sane decision which may be equal to any other process.

Some decide on cremation for the sake of economy. In this instance, as we have shown, the family has to be careful if a savings is actually to be realized.

The most damaging reason for cremation is hostility. The survivor may be angry at death, or at the deceased person, or at God, or at someone else. If he selects cremation for that reason, he is possibly in store for an enormous amount of grief later.

Every minister and funeral director has met this person sooner or later. He can't accept bereavement as a natural part of life. Unable to face it, he tries to eliminate the body as soon as possible. "Get rid of it. I don't want to see it." For him there will be no service, no viewing. He simply doesn't want to talk about it. This person has deep-seated troubles that will probably get worse unless he will let someone get close to him and loosen the valves. If he can't let off steam, he will soon blow sky high.

A second cousin to the "death-hater" is the "self-defacer." He instructs his family to cremate him as a personal put-down. He wants to be blotted out. Cremation represents a complete erasure. It is what he feels he really deserves. This person has serious problems and probably could benefit from counseling. He would do himself a favor if he would seek some temporary help.

If cremation is to be considered seriously, it will represent a wide departure for most of us. Some members of our families may take the idea painfully. They may even suffer from exaggerated visions of bodies burning. They could picture the body going through extreme agony.

The easiest way to adapt to the idea is to begin discussions early. One considering it should seek to convince his family that he has sound reasons for wanting cremation. He must assure them that the idea is not a prank or an attempt to shock. He must let them ask questions and then seek to provide accurate answers.

The time to discuss cremation is not thirty minutes after the relative has died. The survivors may find it difficult to adjust to what strikes them as bizarre and possibly pagan.

An excited funeral director blurted this out to a group of ministers: "If you ask me, the whole thing is a communist plot. First they make an attack on our funeral practices and now they try to get rid of smoking."

This man was serious. He really was. And unfortunately it's common to be suspicious of change. For some reason, most of us don't adjust readily. But that doesn't make every new wrinkle communistic or pagan.

For centuries we have treated cremation as un-Christian. But what biblical basis is there for rejecting it? Or does God leave funeral practices entirely up to the individual?

Protestants have swung from adamant opposition to official indifference. While many still reject cremation for themselves, they see few theological difficulties in it. The Roman Catholic Church had previously voiced total rejection of the practice. In recent years they have specified burial as preferable but cremation as acceptable. Jewish communities are altering their funeral practices, but they still treat cremation as a fringe method.

The Scriptures don't recommend any particular funeral practice. We see a cartload of examples but almost nothing in the way of command or even preference. We merely note entombment as the general procedure under normal circumstances, from Moses to Jesus Christ.

Except in a few cases such as Jacob, Jewish bodies were not normally embalmed. After the wrapping and perfuming, most bodies were placed in tombs where they were allowed to decompose. Sometime later, the bones were collected into a two-foot-by-foot-and-a-half box called an ossuary. The body was then stored in the tomb in this box. Except for crushing the bones, the results were similar to cremation.

When the burning of bodies does occur in the Bible, it is usually connected with punishment (2 Kings 23:20; Joshua 7:25). But again, this was not by command from God.

We can say two things about the biblical concept of cremation. First, cremation was known throughout Judeo-Christian history. Julius Caesar was cremated. The Greeks cremated and the Romans burned the bodies of Christians to try to prevent resurrection.

Second, Christians, though aware of the practice, did not choose it. The option was open to the early believers but they rejected it. The Jewish Mishna forbade cremation as idolatry.

These are the historical facts. However, these facts do not constitute a doctrine. They are merely arguments from silence. Because Christians did not cremate in the first century does not mean they cannot in the twentieth. Many of our funeral practices do not match those of early Christians, but there is no necessity that they do.

Every Christian must decide the question for himself. Without a specific command or instruction he apparently is free to choose for himself. If the method of body disposal were vital, God would surely have given us guidance on the subject.

Some believers reject cremation on the grounds of the resurrection. However, if God can resurrect those destroyed by lions, if he can reclaim martyrs burned at the stake, if he can recall those blown apart during war, cremation is no obstacle. Belief in the resurrection does not need to flinch at any condition of the body. Most bodies of Christians have completely decayed over the centuries.

Funeral traditions come and go like any other fad or practice. We no longer drape mirrors in black, and most people do not hang wreaths on their doors. American funerals are changing and some of the innovations may be for the best. Cremation could someday be a leading preference in the United States. Greater numbers of Christians may find it desirable in the century ahead.

If you want more information about cremation write to: Cremation Association of America, 1620 West Belmont, Fresno, CA 93728.

SEVEN
DONATING
YOUR ORGANS
AND BODY

It isn't fair to talk about transplants without meeting John Thomas of Aurora, Nebraska. John is somewhere in his forties and has a smile as warm as a muffin. Not too long ago his kidneys stopped doing their job. His body began to fill with poison and a solution had to be found quickly.

The immediate answer was use of a dialysis machine to clean out his system. The device would fight uremia and keep him alive. The machine meant hope, but it wasn't the New Jerusalem. Three times a week John had to report to a hospital. Each visit meant five hours connected to a pumping box.

As weeks dragged into months the process became increasingly difficult. Fight faded into resignation. If something drastic didn't happen, John's future didn't look bright.

How does a person support his family and keep his job with this kind of schedule? Realistically he can't. John worked for a compassionate company. They stretched their hearts to help. But how long could this last?

Depression is a cruel ghoul. It started to make regular treks into John's life. But he was fortunate. He was able to get off the machine after three months. Many people have to stay on it for years. Some youth are on the box with little hope of ever being free.

John's freedom came with the news that a kidney transplant was available. A person in another state had died and donated his organ. John was to report immediately for surgery.

He needed only one kidney. (One can do the job well.) Soon he was walking around. In a couple of months he was working part time. It has been a full year and a half since John's new lease on life. He now works like a termite and enjoys his family more than ever.

But the mobile home administrator isn't kidding himself. Anyone who carries a borrowed kidney is aware of the problems he faces. The biggest obstacle is the possibility that his body may eventually reject the organ sewed into it. Months or even years after the installation his body may react powerfully and render the kidney useless. Because he lives with that shadow, every day is worth more to him.

To combat rejection, John takes a parade of pills every day. He is aware that some people have adverse effects from the medicine. Cancer is slightly more frequent among kidney recipients.

John Thomas knows all of this and still he is as happy as an otter on an ice pond. He's alive. He's at liberty. He's thankful to both man and God. John believes in kidney transplants.

Thirty years ago there would have been practically no hope for patients like John. When World War 2 ended, experiments were being made, but the medical procedure was infantile at best. Now, thanks to the research of Doctors Hufnagel, Hume, and Landsteiner, thousands of successful transplants have been accomplished. Some doctors still consider them too experimental; yet many people would be dead except for a transferred kidney.

In this discussion we will consider mainly kidneys, but many other organs can be transplanted. The most common transplant is the normal blood transfusion. Some form of transference is also being done with skin, eye corneas, liver, heart, teeth, pancreas, bone marrow, glands, inner ear parts, blood vessels, ova, tendons, and more. Many of these are so new they still strike some of us like science fiction. But thousands of people are living enjoyable lives because donors have given up their organs.

The Christian tries to sort out the facts and is left with unprecedented decisions. We'd like to turn to a passage in James and get a direct command about transplants. But since we can't, let's try to check out some Christian principles and ask God for guidance.

Should we donate our organs or attempt to keep our body intact? Are we entering areas where man in fact has no right to go? Is it our Christian service to contribute what we can to desperate patients?

Two decisions are essential before we make up our minds. The first consideration is our opinion of the Christian's body. We should be careful to read the chapter in this book dealing with the subject "The Christian View of the Body." Until we settle the question of the body, we will have difficulty knowing what to do with our organs.

If we can agree that the body should be respected but not worshiped, our decision will be easier. Once we accept the inevitable uselessness of the cadaver, our choices may crystallize.

The second principle to consider is love for our brother and neighbor. When John wrote about Jesus Christ, he said, "Having loved his own in the world, he now showed them the full extent of his love" (John 13:1, NIV). We should want to find ways of expressing our love in tangible form. Words are weak when compared with action.

Kidney transplants are accepted from both living and deceased donors. However, in recent years non-relative living donors are being discouraged. They offer no advantage over a cadaver organ, and many doctors would prefer to take no chances with a healthy person.

This attitude changes if we are talking about a close living relative. A parent, brother, or sister is the best possible kidney donor. Their common blood and tissue type often sharply reduce the odds of rejection.

The most successful kidney transplant so far came from a relative. Twenty years ago an identical twin received a kidney from her sister. The recipient not only continues to function normally but has given birth to three children.

If a patient gets a kidney from a relative, his odds of survival are excellent. Ninety percent will not suffer rejection during the first year. Eighty percent are functioning after the second year. However, qualified relatives are few, and there is certainly some risk to them. Contributors have to be available to make up the gap.

Many wonder if there actually is an urgent need for donated kidneys. According to the National Kidney Foundation, 8,000 people are presently waiting for kidneys. Their future will be difficult at best, but it is seriously gloomy if they cannot get an organ.

Amazing as it may seem, the recipient doesn't need two kidneys. One will work quite acceptably, performing all the functions necessary to sift out poisons.

Some of the 8,000 patients we have mentioned have had transplants before. A few have tried as many as four or five. They are still looking for the right one which their body will not reject.

If some kidneys don't work, how do we know ours won't be wasted? This is such an important business that no organ is treated lightly. If a kidney is diseased or for some other reason cannot function, then naturally it isn't put into a patient. But otherwise every attempt is made.

Careful contacts are kept between the 132 transplant centers in the United States. If someone dies in another state his kidney may be shipped immediately to a waiting recipient. John Thomas doesn't know who donated his kidney. That information is kept in confidence. However, he does have reason to believe it was brought in from a distance of 500 miles.

An organ can be kept for seventy-two hours after it is removed. It is preserved at a low temperature. Special police cars and airplanes are often used to guarantee swift transport.

Even in cases in which the recipient's body rejects the kidney, the donor's family knows they have tried. They are not normally told who got the organ, but they can be satisfied that the donated organ gave someone a chance for a normal life.

Most Christian groups have no official reservation about donations or procedures. Yet some individuals go to extremes and risk their own children's lives rather than allow them to accept a blood transfusion. The majority of people see the practical necessity of such procedures and recognize them as basic expressions of love.

Occasionally someone still raises the old objection about crossing races. Everyone should be completely assured that race and color have no bearing on transplants. There is no difference between a white man's kidney and a black man's. Many readers will think it is silly to bring up this notion. The only reason we do is because some people still believe old fallacies.

In all candor we must mention the view of objecting physicians. Not every doctor considers organ transplants a valid medical practice. Some look at it as far too experimental. These are honest and intelligent professionals, and their arguments are not without credence. They say that the person who receives a kidney is launching onto a sea of difficulty. His life will never be exactly "normal." His life expectancy cannot presently be considered great. A surgeon in Detroit declared, "I only hope these people are being told the truth from the beginning. A transplant is not a cure. Life is going to be tough."

Proponents merely reply, "But they are alive." With progress the procedure should improve. Presently, advances are slow, but there is hope for further progress.

Without a transplant, a patient must remain dependent on the dialysis machine. He has no choice. Others have a choice and still select the machine. We cannot say that every patient is better off with a transplant; it depends on the person. But if you ask John Thomas, the answer is as sharp as a whip crack. He thanks God for a transplant and the hope it represents.

One of the more amazing but less publicized transplants is skin grafting. This has become a highly successful art and a fairly common practice. Thousands of individuals are living normal lives because donor skin was available.

Some skin transplants are conducted purely for emergency work. The patient may be burned on 80 percent of his body and need immediate help to stabilize him. Later other skin is used to make permanent repairs.

These transplants, like those of kidneys, can be accepted from either a living or deceased person. Skin grafting is an ancient practice. It was carried out successfully even before Christ was born. However, it was done only from one part of a person's body to another part. Today one individual can contribute skin to someone else. If the donor is a living person, his own skin normally rebuilds.

If an individual wants to give transplants at his death, he should make his desire known in advance. Special donor cards are available from the addresses at the end of this chapter. In twenty-six states a potential donor can have a special note placed on his driver's license.

A word of warning, which is repeated other places in this book: It is unwise and unfair to ask your survivors to do something strange or offensive to them. Make your wishes clear, but do not try to lock them into anything bizarre.

In no area are transplants more successful than with eye corneas. Over 10,000 people have received a new outer lens for their eye and are enjoying excellent vision. A person who would have been seriously handicapped can now enjoy a fully sighted life.

The donor does not need to have good vision in order for his transplant to be used. The person who receives the cornea might receive 20-20 vision from a cornea whose previous owner had poor eyesight.

If we choose to give our organs to medical recycling we should not worry about it affecting our funeral. Practically any and all organs can be donated without changing the appearance of the body. In the process of embalming and preparation for burial, the organs will naturally become useless.

People often wonder about heart transplants. These may be acutely controversial to some who think of the heart as being the real personality. The future of these transplants is unclear.

But their risk and rate of rejection should not be allowed to cloud the issues. Other transplants are far less shaky and extremely beneficial.

Transplants of any nature can be outrageously expensive. In the past some kidney transfers have cost $100,000. Now the cost has dropped dramatically. Since 1972, Social Security amendments provide the benefits of Medicare to most U. S. kidney transplant candidates. The cost of removing an organ is paid for by the receiving family or by an involved organization.

If we volunteer to donate organs, what guarantee do we have they will not be taken too soon? It's an ugly question, but one which haunts the back of many minds.

As in all medical procedures, we are dependent on a doctor's personal and professional ethics. His purpose is to preserve life. He cannot ignore one life to extend another. The physician is sworn to protect your life.

Medical schools remain in constant need of bodies for their classes to study. The cadaver cannot have undergone an autopsy or contain a disease. It is hard for training doctors to learn effectively if they do not actually have a body to work on. It is a little bit like taking mechanic courses without a car.

Despite rumors to the contrary, bodies are greatly needed. Doctors, dentists, nurses, and other health practitioners must have cadavers in order to learn well. Officials in control assure the donors that the body will be treated with respect. After its use, a dignified, nondenominational service is held for the funeral.

Eye and kidney transplants are normally encouraged by the medical school. The body is still usable after those organs are removed. No money can be paid for a body, but in most cases there will be no expense to the family either. In some situations the family may have to pay for the initial delivery of the body, but in other cases this is not true. It is best to check with the medical school for particulars.

In some areas body donation has received a bad image. We have thought of criminals and paupers leaving their cadavers to science. Often the opposite is true. Many times it is the well

71

educated and the successful who choose this type of service.

The age or youth of the body makes almost no difference. In most cases it can be used over a considerable period. Often the bodies are studied for one year and sometimes for two or more.

It is also possible to donate a relative's body. However, the most important consideration is to discuss the prospect with the person while he is comparatively well.

If you choose to donate your body, it is important to fill out the necessary forms and carry a donor's card. Some make a mistake by including their instructions in their wills, which may not be read until after the funeral.

The Christian must pivot on the question of faith. Does it demonstrate strong belief in God to bury the body intact? Or do we demonstrate faith by other action, knowing the entire body does not need to be buried? It is a personal question which must be answered individually.

Whichever route is selected, the facts should be made available. Transplants are being successfully accomplished. People are gaining a new life through the use of deceased persons' organs. Some of these lives are restricted and some are short, but they are extended.

It is also true that thousands are waiting for their chance. Some are two-year-old children who can't see or who are dependent on a machine.

As Dr. Benjamin Barnes of the Interhospital Bank Committee says, people are waiting in line for needed organs. "The urgent need for all organs is greatly underappreciated by the public."

There is no need to sign a separate card for each organ you would like to donate. The National Kidney Foundation has a "Uniform Donor Card." The donor can indicate a specific organ, give permission for all needed organs, or donate the entire body. He can also note any limitations at the bottom of the card. This will give survivors a clear statement of how you feel about donations.

Before any final decisions are made, here are some addresses you might want to write:

National Kidney Foundation
116 East 27th Street
New York, NY 10016

Transplantation and Immunology Branch of the National
Institute of Allergy and Infectious Diseases
Bethesda, MD 20014

End-Stage Renal Disease Program
Bureau of Quality Assurance
Health Services Administration
U.S. Department of Health, Education and Welfare
5600 Fishers Lane
Rockville, MD 20852

Eye Bank Association of America
3195 Maplewood Avenue
Winston-Salem, NC 27103
(or see a member of your local Lions Club)

Anatomical Donations
(For a local or regional address, write your local medical
school, consult your phone book, or call your doctor.)

EIGHT
WHAT ABOUT
AUTOPSIES?

She was a cheerleader at her high school and she was packed with energy. One evening after practice, Chris went to a friend's house where four or five girls were finishing their homework. After a fun time she returned home tired. Bidding her family good-night she went to bed at the regular hour. During her sleep Chris quietly died.

Her stunned family was faced with swirling and difficult decisions to make in a hurry. Their shock didn't make it any easier to think. Should they accept the doctor's diagnosis or look deeper for the cause? Was it possible Chris had died from a rare virus which could bring down her friends too? Should they agree to an autopsy which might produce the exact answer? What would an autopsy mean to the body of their teenager, and how might it affect them? There was so much to consider just two hours after the shocking death of their oldest daughter.

Autopsies are a mystery to most of us. A quick trip to the library offers little helpful information. Yet it is an important decision which many of us may eventually face. The better we understand it now, the more hope we have of making an intelligent choice tomorrow.

Briefly stated, an autopsy is the dissecting of a human body.

In most instances it involves only selected parts. In some cases practically every inch is opened and closely examined. When the time comes to make a decision it will be necessary to know which process is being considered.

A few people refuse to consider an autopsy because of religious beliefs. They look at it as a mutilation of the body. A small number of Protestant groups take this position, along with some of the more conservative Jewish organizations. Those who protest on religious grounds normally point to Deuteronomy 21:23: "His body shall not remain on the tree overnight. You must bury him the same day, for anyone hanging on a tree is cursed of God. Don't defile the land the Lord your God has given you" (TLB).

Most people deserve respect for their attempt to apply the Bible correctly. Those who find this verse prohibitive of autopsy should be respected. However, there is no reason for us all to accept this interpretation of this verse. The Old Testament directives concerning body care must be understood in their context.

The early Israelites faced hygiene and disease problems with which they could not cope. Immediate burial was the only option in many cases. If we were to adhere to all the ancient laws we would stone our children for disobedience. Whatever our views on autopsies, this verse will not be critical for most of us. We need to consider the practical and current aspects of autopsy.

Most Catholic, Protestant, and some Jewish groups have no argument on theological grounds. The issue has to be resolved in other arenas. And to face this question squarely we need to discover the purpose of an autopsy.

Sometimes there is the need to determine the cause of death. A person may die suddenly and without warning. It could be important for various reasons to discover the cause. The information may put minds at ease and spare them years of wondering. Ascertainment of the cause could protect other family members from the same disease. One survey of 1,000 autopsies showed many disagreements with the first reason given for death. If there is any serious doubt, this process might clear it up.

A second reason for an autopsy is research. By studying a disease and its effects, doctors often are able to help prevent others' illness or death. A gentleman dying from cancer in Omaha specifically requested an autopsy. He wanted to help those who followed him. Pathologists could possibly learn how to fight early deaths in the future.

This is a frequent reason for a request by hospital physicians who know with reasonable certainty what ended the patient's life. By removing the lungs of the emphysema victim, for example, they could come closer to an understanding and a cure. Several major developments in preventing heart disease have been accomplished because of autopsies. Bronchitis has been reevaluated and classified through this process. Sometimes those investigations can be made through a limited rather than a complete autopsy.

A large percentage of autopsies are conducted to solve legal problems. Criminal investigations are frequently dependent on a thorough dissecting of the body. Cases are solved regularly by forensic pathologists. Several intriguing books have been written to describe this fascinating science. Insurance companies are understandably interested in discovering the exact cause of death. Sometimes physicians are protected from accusations of malpractice by the evidence gathered in an autopsy.

Autopsies are necessary at some level to help train doctors and dentists. Otherwise it is comparable to studying medicine by correspondence. Often donated bodies are collected to meet this need.

The findings of pathologists contribute measurably to community health. They can indicate the currect trends of diseases which are claiming lives. Pathologists argue forcefully that this is the only way to collect dependable data.

Some physicians will push for autopsies to help gather reusable parts. Heart valves, arteries, bone, cartilage, and skin are only a few of the usuable materials, not counting the more obvious: cornea, kidneys, lungs, and liver. Often man-made materials such as Kuntscher nails, Vitallium screws, and heart valve prostheses are reclaimed too.

The person who performs autopsies regularly can give a host of reasons to do it. Not all doctors will agree. More than one feels it is overdone and hardly productive. This is why it is important to be informed and have a physician whom you respect.

If a decision is to be made, whose job is it? There is a fairly clear-cut line of authority which most states recognize.

If a crime or suicide is suspected, the local medical examiner or coroner takes immediate control of the body. He has the authority to order an autopsy without consent from the relatives. The same thing is true if death was caused by drugs, alcoholism, or any other suspicious factor. Private citizens can protest this, but usually to no avail.

When the state has no claim on a body, the first choice goes to the individual. The deceased can leave a written preference. Possibly he is tremendously opposed to an autopsy. On the other hand he may consider it a noble contribution to humanity. In most areas his clear wishes must be honored. If he feels strongly about it, he would be wise to discuss it with his family.

After the deceased, the line of authority follows this pattern:

1. Surviving spouse
2. Children, if of age
3. Grandchildren, if of age
4. Parents
5. Brothers and sisters
6. Grandparents
7. Aunts and uncles
8. Cousins
9. Friends, if they are responsible for the funeral arrangements.

The status of a common-law spouse will differ considerably from state to state.

A careful pathologist will try to get several signatures, to protect himself. Normally the family does not bear the expense unless they request the autopsy.

It is common to think an autopsy is an autopsy. This is not really the case. There are several ways to perform one. The relatives should know exactly how far the procedure will go before agreeing.

If the family raises no restrictions to an autopsy, the entire process is likely to be followed. The chest and abdominal cavities may be examined and the brain may be removed.

When additional procedures are to be followed, such as exploration of the face, neck, hands, or spinal column, special permission should be secured. Otherwise a pathologist will not bother with these under normal conditions. This is also true of the removal of the eyes (*Current Methods of Autopsy Practice*, p. 301).

Consequently, the family has the right to restrict the autopsy. In discussion with a physician they can draw the boundaries and write them on the permission certificate. If the pathologist feels the guidelines are too limiting he may refuse to do the autopsy. Both he and the family have their options. The survivors should know this and not be afraid to exercise them.

This would also be a good time to decide whether or not to donate the individual's organs for transplants. If the survivors want them buried with the body, they have a right to this preference also.

Any qualified physician, surgeon, pathologist, or toxicologist can perform an autopsy. Those who have special training and experience, such as pathologists, may be better qualified. In criminal cases, a forensic pathologist has the most expertise.

An autopsy can be an expensive procedure. Before agreeing to one, the family would be wise to ask who will pay for it.

Traditionally, pathologists and funeral directors have had their differences. Morticians often feel the physician goes too far and makes the body difficult to prepare. Pathologists believe directors cannot appreciate the job which has to be done. In recent years there have been calls for greater cooperation between the two.

Autopsies remain in the uneasy middle. Their defenders insist they are making enormous contributions to science. Their detractors believe too many are done with too little results.

NINE
FUNERAL
DIRECTORS
ARE HUMAN

Most of us have mixed emotions when we meet funeral directors. We are glad to see them, but we hate to see them. They represent help and service, but they also suggest loss and pain.

Fortunately for all of us, the overwhelming majority of directors are kind and considerate. They maintain a high level of professionalism and are solid contributors to the community. During years of working with them in planning and conducting services, I found only one who was gruff and inconsiderate. There aren't many groups which hold such a high level of consistency. I remember only one family which expressed thorough disappointment with the funeral director.

These observations aren't terribly scientific. Nevertheless I think they may represent the feelings of the majority of the American public. Surveys prove repeatedly that over 90 percent of our families are pleased with the funeral service they get. Read that sentence again so it will sink in.

Many of us would like some adjustments. Most of us do not like the cost. We also are not thrilled with the cost of homes, cars, refrigerators, doctors, and football games.

Over a five-year period there are approximately ten million funerals in the United States. During that time the Federal

Trade Commission has received a total of almost 1,000 complaints. This amounts to 200 per year or one complaint to the F.T.C. per 10,000 funerals. This number becomes almost nonexistent when we consider the adverse publicity the industry has received in the past decade.

Management Horizon, Inc., conducted a survey for Wilbert, Inc., and came to the same conclusion: "While the vast majority are satisfied with funeral service, this study shows that there is a small majority who, at the basic level, strongly feel that funerals are not helpful and that they do not want a funeral. While the percentage with those strong feelings may be small (3.1 percent) it takes only a few to express their feelings and perhaps try to impose them on others."

Memorial Societies have been in gear for several years and apparently are growing in numbers. However, their impact on the total population is fractional. The facts seem to indicate an overall acceptance of the funeral director in his present role. While uncomfortable with the cost, most of us see the director as a definite help in a time of distress.

As indicated in an earlier chapter, there is a slight trend toward cremation (about 8 percent) but even here the funeral director's responsibility is unchanged. A considerable percentage of cremation funerals still prefer the traditional service before disposal.

The funeral director still holds a respected position in our society. Many have worked hard to gain a high standing in their communities. The average director's education may vary from state to state, but often consists of college and professional school. Half of the states insist on a year or two of college. The emphasis is on chemistry, business, and English. All states demand one year of mortuary school. Approximately thirty mortuary schools dot the nation. On top of the formal training a one-year apprenticeship is normally required. The individual must then pass an examination administered by the state board.

The 23,000 funeral homes in the United States average fewer

than 100 funerals per year. The country has about one funeral home for each 10,000 people.

Most funeral homes have a long-established record. The average has served its community for forty-five years. Some funeral homes are in the fourth generation of the family.

Presently the average funeral home employee has an annual salary comparable to that of a schoolteacher. The owner's income may be twice that amount, but his financial investment is considerable. Normally he uses a large building, several vehicles, and some expensive equipment. He also has a large investment in merchandise. The owner takes a financial risk, as do most small businessmen in our nation.

There is no reason to pity them; they make a living. There may be no reason to envy them, either; most will never become wealthy.

Unfortunately, some people resent the fact that funeral directors make a living from deaths. They feel directors are ghouls who benefit from the tragedies of others. In reality we cannot expect funeral homes to operate without adequate compensation. Maybe there are things we can do to help bring down the costs. Possibly we can alter our funeral practices. But we cannot deny the practitioner his rightful place in American society.

Some directors have been asked so often about prices and practices that they have become reluctant to discuss their occupation. It is too bad. The more information and education, the better it will be for everyone involved.

Jeanette Pickering, who is mentioned elsewhere in this book, is a funeral director in Lebanon, Missouri. She has taken a healthy, open attitude toward the public. Mrs. Pickering writes a regular question-answer column in a local newspaper. This way she gets to know what bothers the public most about funerals, and has a good forum for reply.

Interested people have written in to ask her about making pre-funeral arrangements. Why don't you advertise your funeral service? How do you answer questions about death?

Do flowers really help a grieving family? Will a donation to the eye bank disfigure a body? Why do all funerals seem the same? Mrs. Pickering creates an atmosphere of trust rather than secrecy. She is not embarrassed by the vocation. Both of her sons have elected to enter the same profession.

It is often difficult to remember how much good is done by the unheralded heroes of some professions. We take lightly the courageous feats performed by the police or local firemen. It is just as easy to forget the dedicated service given sacrificially by funeral directors.

On November 6, 1977, an earthen dam collapsed and sent a raging wall of water racing across the campus of the Toccoa (Georgia) Bible College. In a short time thirty-nine people were dead, twenty-two of them under the age of fifteen.

Before most of the nation had heard of the disaster, Jerry Whitlock, director of a funeral home in Toccoa, was quietly at work. Soon many other directors called to volunteer assistance. By midnight two nearby directors had arrived and started to help.

As the bodies arrived, the massiveness of the tragedy became apparent. There was no water or electrical power available. When the water was finally reconnected it was too contaminated to use. Fifty-gallon drums had to be filled and brought in.

The funeral directors worked through the night and families began arriving at 8:30 to identify the bodies. Morticians met the relatives as they came in and tried to help each one. They checked bodies as often as every five minutes for purge problems; otherwise there could be seepage from the bodies.

Despite their familiarity with death, this situation took its toll on the directors. The combination of so many, so young, was hard to grasp. As one mortician said, he cried more during those twenty-four hours than he had during the previous twenty-four years.

The local director, Jerry Whitlock, tried to talk to each family. If they wanted to use his funeral home, he was glad to assist. If not, there would be no charges at all for the service done so far.

Those who worked through the ordeal were a great help to the survivors when they most needed them. The student body and staff at Toccoa Bible College also made a deep impression on the directors, who were tremendously moved by the calm faith of these Christians.

These aspects of the funeral business are often left untold. Few of us stop to think of the quiet role they play during personal loss. In some areas funeral homes are taking aggressive and positive steps toward informing the public.

The Blake-Lamb Funeral Home in Chicago has developed several innovative approaches to assisting the grieving. After a funeral they mail a letter to the family offering the services of their library. They keep a generous selection of books and pamphlets which deal with different aspects of grief.

Two weeks after the funeral someone from the home calls on the family. She takes a collection of literature with her and will leave whatever the survivors want. It is a funeral business but it is also a caring service.

Rather than being hesitant to discuss their practices, this organization looks for ways to educate the public. They offer speakers to all kinds of organizations, such as hospitals, churches, schools, and senior citizen groups. Special films are available to grade school and junior high classes. Confident they have a service to offer, they are not afraid to be open about it.

One of the most helpful programs offered by funeral homes is their provision of seminars for clergymen. In most cases the seminars do not degenerate into propaganda sessions. Such capable speakers as Dr. Elisabeth Kubler-Ross and Rabbi Earl Grollman are among their resource people.

Funeral directors are becoming acutely aware of their role in grief counseling. Some have seen their role as taking care of the mechanics and allowing someone else to deal with the personal problems. This concept is changing for many morticians.

The National Funeral Directors Association has given financial grants for professional studies of grief and its effects. The material gleaned from this research has been rechanneled into funeral homes and other involved groups. Directors are learning communication skills to help the bereaved.

Some cynics will protest that this is a purely commercial venture. By being kind they are trying to drum up future business. This is a harsh accusation which puts the director in an impossible position. Psychologists help people and also benefit personally. So do doctors, dentists, and clergymen. Many funeral directors are going an extra mile to help people; sometimes they gain financially from it. That does not make them charlatans or ghouls.

Grief has become the silent killer in our society. The death rate among widows is 50 percent higher during the first two years after the spouse dies. Often physical and mental health degenerate rapidly after a partner's death.

Robert Nink, executive director of the Illinois Funeral Directors Association, throws out a realistic challenge concerning grief. Writing in *American Funeral Director*, he calls for bold research. Does the traditional funeral really offer greater comfort to the family than other forms? Are those who selected body donations or immediate disposition or even cremation really worse off? Do they have greater difficulty adjusting to grief?

This attitude demonstrates an open mind to find out what is best. Possibly crusaders overstated the case on several sides of the funeral question.

It would also be interesting to study surviving Christians' ability to cope. Does their faith enable them to accept death better? We have nothing to fear by an impartial analysis.

Joseph Bayly summed up the average funeral director well in this statement: "But the funeral director is a man, with all the feelings and capacities of most human beings. More than other men, except for pastors and other religious advisors, and doctors in certain specialties, he lives with sorrow. He is usually able to help us in our moments of grief—moments when the burdens of decision weigh heaviest" (*The View from a Hearse*, p. 69, David C. Cook, 1969).

Funeral directors are often quality assets to a community. They generally conduct themselves in a highly professional manner. Frequently directors are members of fraternal and service organizations such as Lions, Rotary, or Kiwanis. It isn't uncommon for them to be civic leaders and highly active in their local churches. In many cases they do not exist on the borders of their society but are close to the heart of it. This wouldn't be worth mentioning except for the fact that others are painting them as criminals and perpetrators of dark deeds. If the accusations are occasionally true, the opposite is overwhelmingly common.

To begin to appreciate the work of the funeral director we need to recognize the void they fill. Let us imagine them to be removed from the professional ranks of our community. Are we prepared to return to having family and friends "undertaking" our funeral arrangements? Are we content to have them fix the body and build the coffin? Are they to pack the deceased in ice if we want to wait a couple of days until Aunt Anna can arrive? The good old days may sound good in pioneer books and television shows, but most of us are in no hurry to return to them.

Certain people look down on funeral directors as persons of low calling. Fortunately this isn't true everywhere, especially where the public is better informed.

A community in Brooklyn, New York, was expecting considerable expense as they collected money in the neighborhood. A thirteen-year-old boy had climbed high into a tree, evidently to steal apples. When he accidently touched two electrical wires, 208 volts raced through his body. His hands were blackened and molded to the wires.

The neighbors wanted to raise money to give the boy a good funeral. When they carried their funds to the local funeral home, they were in for a shock. Michael DeLuca explained the situation to the covey of citizens. As a policy the DeLuca Funeral Home never asks money for a child's funeral.

A few days later the *New York Daily News* carried the story of the mortician's generous spirit. In their Brooklyn neighborhood there is a great deal of respect for a funeral director. There would be elsewhere if more people realized the magnanimous attitude of many directors.

Some readers will think this is merely an isolated case. However, this is a fairly frequent occurrence among funeral directors. The Federal Trade Commission in its critical investigation of the industry made this observation about funeral homes in Washington, D.C.:

"It is important to note that many D.C. mortuaries handle some hardship cases at prices lower than those in the chart. This survey did not cover the prices paid in such special situations, since the funeral director charges each needy family only what it can afford, rather than his regularly offered prices" (F.T.C. "Survey of Funeral Prices in the District of Columbia," p. 5).

This attitude is borne out again in such tragedies as the battered boy found near Ashland, Ohio. He had evidently died from child abuse at the age of two or three. When authorities were unable to identify the child, the local funeral director assumed responsibility for the body. Thirty people attended the service for the nameless child. The morticians had donated a casket and vault for the funeral.

Generally funeral directors are warmed with a healthy sense of humor. When you face death and heartache, a funny bone is essential to self-preservation. After all, there is no way to guess what odd request will come.

In Sussex, England, a twenty-four-year-old motorcycle enthusiast tested morticians' humor and sanity at the same time. Dave Phillips wanted to buy a regular coffin to take with him. No one had died, he tried to explain. He wanted a casket to convert into a sidecar for his motorcycle. Dave's wife, Jane, was willing to ride in it as they toured around town.

There is no record of how many funeral directors thought this was funny. We do know that at least fourteen morticians turned him down before he was able to buy one. The price was $270.

If some people find humor in coffins, others have decided to make a profit from the fact. A few cities now have a "Rent-a-Casket" business. A gentleman in St. Louis bought a smoke-damaged casket for $250 and put an ad in the paper to rent it. The one small ad brought him 100 inquiries; it rents for $50 a day.

Caskets are being used for birthday parties and in some cases filled with martinis. A minister in Wichita used a coffin to illustrate the certainty of death and to call men to repentance.

Other groups not only rent caskets but sell them. A lady in Los Angeles purchased a casket and converted it into a wine rack. Still others might want to buy a $300 mahogany model and make a china cabinet. They are sometimes lined with tin and used as planters. One individual has covered the top of one with glass and uses it for a coffee table.

A funeral director does not always lead the dour "Digby O'Dell" life his stereotype calls for. He may not be thrilled with these uses for caskets, he may not be excited about memorial societies, but he is learning more and more to laugh at himself.

If these requests seem odd, consider the one received by Canadian funeral directors. In 1952 David Brown retired from funeral service and started a strange collection. For seventeen years Brown traveled through Canada and gathered 50,000 embalming fluid bottles. He then stacked the containers and built his home out of the empty bottles. This is not a toy or show home; Brown constructed a real one with circular rooms and modern interior. He never intended to make it a showroom or conversation piece, but people came to look. Despite the rise in costs for building materials, embalming fluid bottles are not likely to catch on. Maybe morticians are just as human as anyone.

While most people ask for a conventional funeral, there are enough exceptions to prevent boredom. A wealthy gentleman in Hollywood, Florida, has as odd a request as anyone.

Throughout his life this man of means has given heavily to churches and charities. He definitely feels his good deeds will earn him a place in heaven. Consequently, when he dies a key to St. John's Cathedral will be placed in his casket. He figures the key will come in handy and can possibly open some other doors later.

He will probably get his key, since funeral directors generally try to accommodate. Unfortunately the directors can't guarantee how far the key will get him.

Sometimes morticians end up in the middle, as they did in Harrogate, England. A man in his middle forties died and left an unusual request. He wanted to be buried with his motorcycle. The funeral directors wanted to please, but this did seem a bit much. The cyclist's wife vetoed the wish of her beloved husband. She didn't want someone digging up the grave just to steal "Nobbly," the motorcycle.

Each day in the life of a funeral director can be different. Some days are fast-paced while others drag. One day there is something amusing; the next day is enough to make the most seasoned man cry. Some days are profitable and others run at a definite loss. One day the director might be uptight from all the criticism; the next he is calm, outgoing, and sacrificing.

Funeral directors are human like the rest of us.

TEN
IMPROVING
THE FUNERAL
BUSINESS

Most funeral directors are kind and thoughtful. Many of the allegations hurled their way are unfair and inflammatory. However, this doesn't mean the industry is without fault. Directors sometimes need to step back and ask themselves some hard questions and evaluate their approach to business. Not everyone outside the industry is an enemy, and not every criticism is unfair.

When Jessica Mitford wrote *The American Way of Death*, she stung the funeral business. It wasn't damaged, but it was sent into a daze. Today many directors are defensive and resent discussing their practices. Others are open and anxious to educate. Those who barricade themselves in their forts only invite deep-seated hostilities. The sharing, approachable director will save the industry a great deal of grief and regulation.

The Federal Trade Commission has been investigating the funeral business for some time. It plans to recommend restrictions. If this comes about, there will be plenty of court litigation for years. Some directors would rather police themselves, and they have voluntarily made necessary changes.

When Jeanette Pickering was installed as president of the Missouri Ninth District funeral directors, she led the group in prayer:

"O God, bless this small group of your servants.

"Lord, we know we are among the select few who have been chosen by you to care, comfort, and assist those who have been weakened by death. We humbly ask for your guidance.

"When we are buffeted about with criticism from those who are unaware of our obligations, give us tolerance. We ask for wisdom to evaluate their words. If their criticism is unfair, instill in us courage and kindness as we confront their disapproval. If their criticism is fair, we ask for strength and wisdom to make the changes necessary to better serve those who grieve.

"In so doing we make manifest your glorious love."

As this attitude prevails, the funeral industry will continue to be upgraded. It is a noble profession which can repair its own potholes.

Probably the first place the funeral director can loosen up is on the state boards. In many states the only people who may serve on them are connected with the funeral industry. These boards issue regulations for funeral homes and cemeteries.

It is easy to understand the reluctance to spread wider. In the first place, most laymen know little about the industry. A second protest is that other professional groups, such as the American Bar Association, govern themselves. However, neither objection is immovable. Laymen can learn the funeral business and the industry can benefit from the consumer. If they get all their advice from professionals, their perspective becomes too limited. Possibly other professional associations also need the same balance on boards and committees.

Jack Kahn, a hearing officer of the Federal Trade Commission, has called the state boards "puppets" of the funeral directors. He has suggested that each board include a minority of funeral personnel. In his opinion these boards have worked to hinder alternate funeral practices. Consumer allegations merit reevaluation by the funeral industry. Their openness can benefit business rather than injure it.

In some cases state funeral boards either prohibit or discourage price advertising. These rigid restrictions should stop so that the individual funeral business can pursue what it thinks best.

If the directors are to be scrutinized by the public, the cemetery industry cannot be ignored. Some cemeteries insist on a vault because they supposedly fear cave-ins. They then may demand that the vault be bought from them. Does this represent an abusive monopoly? Is the consumer being deprived of his rights?

The consumer might be more interested in a concrete box than a vault. This, too, will keep the ground from caving in and is an option that should be presented fairly.

The same cemetery may have restrictive rules concerning markers. Some cemeteries will allow only the markers which they sell. Usually monuments from private companies are less expensive than those sold by the cemetery. At other cemeteries the cost of installation is higher if the marker is purchased independently.

The public should be allowed to resist these practices. The best solution is to shop around. Most of us don't. Sometimes government agencies do. In 1977 the state of Iowa filed against cemetery practices of selling markers. The Attorney General claimed that refusal to accept markers from private companies violated the Iowa Anti-Trust Act. The decree also demanded a uniform reasonable fee for the installation of markers.

Often families are unaware of their options after cremation. In many areas they may do whatever they wish with the ashes. However, some cemeteries and crematories do not tell this to the relatives, because they sell expensive urns and burial plots. Out of our own ignorance we are deprived of our options.

For instance the Cremation Association of North America has prepared a pamphlet on cremation. It is done neatly and consists of questions and answers. One of the questions is "Can cremated remains be scattered?" They take two paragraphs to answer the question and, in my opinion, never do. Such words as "neither practical" and "inconsiderate" poke up, but there is no direct reply. Apparently their desire to sell urns and plots gets in the way of their eagerness to help. The fact is that ashes can be scatttered in most areas, and often are. Credibility is hurt by not saying this straightforwardly.

If the consumer is surprised at the charges in a funeral home, he may be in for even more of a shock at the cemetery. The plot, opening, vault, marker, closing, and perpetual care can be highly expensive. Some cemeteries also charge for endowment care of the marker. For a price they keep the monument in good shape.

When it comes to state funeral laws, the director is in the driver's seat. He is the only one who deals with the subject. The average layman doesn't know all the highway laws, let alone those affecting body disposal. Even the funeral director doesn't know all of the laws, and will often misquote. He tends to remember the ones he likes best.

When the Federal Trade Commission took a survey of funeral homes in the District of Columbia, they asked if caskets were necessary for cremation. Five homes answered it incorrectly and stated that a casket was mandatory. Some are not familiar with the laws.

A state funeral association could do everyone a favor by printing local laws in a pamphlet. They could spell out each regulation and distribute these to civic, fraternal, social, and professional groups. The public relations might prove satisfying. Instead of having a closed image, they could assure the public there is nothing to hide. An individual's options should be spelled out carefully and the director should be available to discuss them. Some take the view of every man for himself. However, this is not in the best tradition or interest of the funeral industry. Openness, frankness, and flexibility are its close friends.

The fact remains that some people do not get what they want because they don't know any better. A concerned funeral director will be careful to clarify all the possibilities which interest the consumer.

Some criticize the funeral director because he profits from grief. The Federal Trade Commission is particularly vocal concerning this "vulnerability." This is a problem in the funeral transaction, worth mentioning in this chapter. However, the blame may be on the wrong foot. The consumer may be victimizing himself.

When the family arrives at the funeral home, they are often as lost as a puppy on the freeway. They have not studied the subject of burials. Many have refused to discuss it even with friends or relatives. Now death has come and there are only a few hours in which to make decisions. There is practically no time to shop around. Few have the desire to discuss alternatives at this late date. If the customer is vulnerable, the director did not make him that way. The griever has failed to drop good anchors before the storm arrived.

The funeral director is obligated to furnish clear price information. Some consumers who have tried to shop around have been totally discouraged by industry personnel. It is easy to understand why directors do not like to quote prices over the telephone. Often the caller doesn't know if he is talking about apples or oranges. It is hard to compare things which have not been seen when there is little time to explain. However, a director could go to considerable effort to please the caller. Rather than giving a flat "no," some salesmanship, politeness, and reasonable leeway may be in order. Prices that indicate general boundaries would prove helpful. A cold "we don't" is bad for the entire industry.

When a director sits down with a potential consumer, complete disclosure and flexibility should be the keys. Complete disclosure includes an itemized list of services and materials. Some directors refuse to do this and offer only a total price to be accepted or rejected. This overall "single unit" pricing and billing method does not allow consumers to consider the costs of the particular services and merchandise they are buying.

Bi-unit pricing means the funeral home divides its price into two figures—one representing the price of the professional services and the second representing the price of the casket.

The most informative is the third method—itemizing prices. From this list the buyer accepts or rejects individual services.

Some directors want laws demanding such lists, while others are pushing for voluntary compliance. The funeral industry would be wise to offer this service. The consumer would be diligent to demand it.

Some consumers are irate when they see the list. The price of an additional processional car shocks them. The cars are expensive for the funeral home to operate, but the consumer should be shown the fee so he may intelligently decide if he wants to make other arrangements for a vehicle.

How much is the charge for use of a funeral tent? Do death certificates cost extra? Does the director charge to phone in the obituary? What is the charge for pallbearers if the home furnishes them? If the director takes care of flowers, is the cost more? If the director advances cash for the grave opening or for the clergyman, will there be an additional fee? We do have a right to know. The wise director will take the initiative and tell us.

The FTC has proposed a rule insisting on some form of itemized listing. Whatever the form, the purchaser should have the right to remove certain items he does not want. In turn the consumer's bill should be reduced accordingly. This does happen in some areas, but in others the funeral directors resist powerfully.

The high cost of funerals is caused in part by the lack of open comparison. If a funeral home doesn't advertise its prices or services, the purchaser has little to go on. Each person who does not shop around is at the mercy of the prices doled out at the time.

Presently there isn't much advertising. Most people select their director from past experience or from the Yellow Pages. Some feel advertising is dehumanizing and will commercialize the industry. Others insist the practice will lead to cut-rate services and deceit. However, many outside the business believe openness and competitiveness will result in better and less expensive service.

The mark-up on caskets is enormous and could be reduced by price comparison. The average funeral director makes a profit of 200 to 300 percent (sometimes higher) on a casket. They believe it is essential to their survival, but it isn't in the best public interest.

Some caskets include mattresses "especially built for comfort." They will match anything we have in our homes. Caskets will often have headrests which lower and raise. These are excellent for the director to use when touching up the face, but they are of minimal value to the deceased or his family.

There is nothing wrong with the selling of caskets. People have a right to select whatever type suits their tastes. Some call their least expensive model the "welfare" casket. The term frightens most consumers off. Besides the right to display and sell caskets, there is also the obligation to be competitive. Of course, some forms of advertisement are brazen, repulsive, and unfair; but a few establishments such as W. W. Chambers of Washington, D.C., have advertised fairly for years. The prices of their services have remained low and their business has prospered.

A simple brochure with pictures, descriptions, and prices could be made available. When someone phones, the director can offer to mail literature immediately. The same thing could apply to their services. Yet many funeral directors appear to be flatly against all innovation in the industry. They are especially opposed to any changes which might lower prices. If this seems too radical a statement, consider the static faced by creative minds in the funeral business.

John Floren and Gene Crowe are two cemetery owners who are trying an innovative approach. They have created a fiberglass coffin which is rustproof and stronger than steel. Under their plan a person has a traditional funeral with all the decorations. However, before the burial the body is transferred from the expensive metal casket into the fiberglass one. The transfer is easy because of the use of a thick cardboard "Slumber Bed" in which it is moved to the fiberglass casket. The metal casket can be used over and over again.

The team of creators believe they can cut funeral costs almost in half. So far, the initial reaction has been favorable on the part of the consumer. Funeral directors do not share in the enthusiasm.

Florida's Board of Funeral Directors considered action against the pair. They call it a "pop-out coffin" and declare that it will give the industry a bad name. Because caskets are the largest profit items in the funeral transaction, few directors want to tamper with them.

Possibly the industry should search its ranks and ask some tough questions. Are they dedicated to service and progress? If not, they leave themselves open to ridicule and contempt. They can earn greater respect by taking the lead in change, rather than fearing it.

In all fairness, other industries are guilty of the same selfishness and stubbornness. Anyone who tries to change certain businesses is greeted with hostility. But all of the companies with this attitude may face organized rebellion.

The casket industry has become a mega-business. Any attempt to tinker with its profits will be fought tenaciously. In 1976, 1,802,492 caksets were sold in the United States; 76,875 tons of steel were used in their manufacturing; 58,364,680 board feet of lumber were made into coffins. These are small figures compared to our total national use of steel and lumber. Yet they indicate a sizable industry and an enormous amount of commerce.

In some areas new approaches are discouraged by the State Board of Funeral Directors. Since these boards are usually served by traditional directors, they may find it difficult to accept new and sometimes threatening ideas. Innovation could still be mutually beneficial. Those who sold the fiberglass caskets were making a 480 percent mark up. Fantastically high! But they were still saving money for the consumer.

Most funeral directors are not dishonest. Their moral principles exceed the average of the general population. However, when they feel threatened, they fight back.

A funeral director in Newark, New Jersey, buried 160 poor people in only thirty-two gravesites. As many as eleven infants were found in one site. For three years he had collected fees from the city under false pretenses. There is little evidence, however, that such cheating is common. And most of the points we discuss in this chapter are not the work of cruel men. Often they are merely cases of playing too close to the vest and lacking flexibility.

In some rural areas excesses do occur because of the lack of competition. More than one funeral director gets a kickback from the local florist. A director may order all the flowers through his office. Some get a 20 percent pay-off from the florist for selecting their shop. Flowers for a large funeral may cost $600. This makes $120 added "income" for the director. Florists are angry at the practice but feel trapped. In the long run the consumer pays for the extra costs. Most directors abhor this practice and may try to weed it out. Others persist and eventually hurt everyone.

One area in which funeral directors have difficulty keeping a balanced outlook is in the area of psychological need. They seem to grab any evidence which suggests man needs our present form of cosmetized body-viewing funeral.

There is documentation to prove that a viewing helps man cope better if he can see the body. However, this is not necessarily true for everyone. In this world billions of people have been buried without our present funeral practices. Their loved ones did not all suffer deep psychological traumas. Our traditional funeral service can be highly therapeutic, but not everyone needs it.

Dr. William M. Lamers, a psychiatrist from Kentfield, California, has written an article supporting the traditional funeral practices. However, the doctor insists it would be unwise to steer the family toward a particular kind of service.

Funeral directors might benefit by loosening up at this point. Instead of assuming too much, they could well back up and offer more options. Instead of waiting to be asked, and then acting indignant when they are, funeral directors could take the initiative. "Would the family like to select cremation? If you do not want a vault, we can recommend a cemetery which does not require one. Since all the relatives are close by, we do not need to embalm the body and can have the funeral in two days."

He can protect his credibility by serving the family with an open attitude. By attempting to prove his methods to be the only psychologically sound practice, he abandons his balance.

A funeral director in Yonkers, New York, has decided to take a progressive approach in light of changing times. He was receiving twenty-four to thirty calls each year for "direct disposition," meaning that they wanted no funeral service. They wanted merely to pick up the body at the hospital and dispose of it immediately, usually through cremation.

Ambrose Havey decided to take a positive step and try to bring these people back into his funeral home. He devised an inexpensive funeral for less than $800 which still had dignity and beauty. Personal services were cut to a minimum, as many of the families wanted. He then created a container which can be placed inside a casket. After the service is completed, the container is removed and the body is buried in it. The body never touches the outer casket, which is reused.

Mr. Havey has found two advantages to his original plan. Since beginning it, he has received only one or two "disposition" calls. The second thing he has discovered is that half of those who come in to discuss the new plan end up buying a traditional "full" funeral. Instead of worrying about changing attitudes, he determined to do something positive, and in the long run everyone is better off. He is now selling his concept as a franchise to funeral directors.

In the United States 20 percent to 30 percent of the population say they want some variation in funeral practices. Whether this percentage will be larger in the future is debatable. However, most people still look to funeral directors and will probably continue to do so. One conclusion of the Wilbert survey of attitudes toward funerals (p. 9) was that future selections of funeral practices would depend in large part on the responses of members of the funeral profession.

There must be a happy middle ground in this debate. The one extreme calls our funeral practices totally pagan and degrading. Overstating their case, they cloud the essential issues. The second extreme claims our practices are particularly godly and essential to our stability and even to our democracy. Both suffer from absurdity.

A sane approach tells us that the funeral director can and often does supply an important function in our society. Because he is flexible and serving, he will continue a respectable role. Because he is a trained professional, he will listen to criticism and not be afraid to adjust.

The need to change can be leveled at practically every profession. Some people claim forty cents out of every auto repair dollar is wasted. Others think lawyers' earnings are abusive. A third group considers doctors overpaid and arrogant. More than one person looks at writers as self-righteous prigs. We all stand in need of self-examination. Our usefulness and satisfaction grow by our ability to change.

Dr. Frank Miller, executive director of the National Selected Morticians, gave sound advice to their sixtieth annual convention in 1977. He reminded the directors that they are often victimized by inbreeding. Because of this they are sometimes unaware of the misinformation which is circulating.

The funeral business can only benefit by listening to valid criticism and making appropriate improvements.

ELEVEN
CHANGES IN
AMERICAN
FUNERALS

If the funeral business was ever dull it certainly hasn't been for the past two decades. On the one side it is a traditional and slow practice. But turn the coin over and we will see myriads of rippling colors and new patterns.

Probably the most drastic change in recent years is the arrival of memorial societies. There are presently 170 groups throughout the United States and Canada, with a total of 600,000 members. The purpose of the societies is to cut funeral costs and present a wide range of options. How effectively they reach their goals is debated by many.

Each local group is run democratically. Membership costs are $10 or $15 for a lifetime. When someone dies, an extra $5 is paid for changes in records.

Memorial societies have been organized by a variety of interested individuals and groups. In some areas churches, ministerial associations, labor organizations, or civic clubs run them. In other places individuals merely start a group from scratch. There is a parent organization in Washington, D.C., with a board of directors.

Ideally the society is impartial and is not trying to promote any type of funeral arrangements. Practically speaking, their literature defends cremation and anatomical donations while casting shadows on the traditional earth burial. Their over-riding concern appears to be economy.

The society encourages its members to select arrangements in advance. They feel that an individual can make a better choice without the stress of grief and guilt. Naturally anyone can change his plans whenever he wants to.

Their brochure claims that participants can save $500 or more on a funeral. They see simplicity as the key to saving money. The best way to attain simplicity is by resisting social pressure. If a person feels free to arrange according to his own moderate taste, he can save considerable money.

The memorial society works with the funeral director in attempting to cut costs. Some directors (perhaps many) see the societies as a threat and infringement. One director characterizes the society's recommendations as "nothing more than an impersonal body disposal."

Questions can be directed to: Continental Association of Funeral and Memorial Societies, Inc., Suite 1100, 1828 L Street, N.W., Washington, DC 20036.

A second trend which appears to be gaining in popularity is the turn to cremation. Whether this increase will continue is open to question.

From 1964 to 1974 the number of cremations doubled in the United States. However, some surveys suggest that the younger generation is *not* indicating a preference for cremation. Those under twenty-five are expressing a negative attitude toward it. The person who selects this type of funeral is more likely to be middle-aged. What these figures say about tomorrow's practices is unclear.

Currently the number of cremations in the United States is not growing rapidly. One reason has to be our Judeo-Christian background. Another is the expense. Cremation-after-viewing is often more costly than a traditional funeral.

In the Wilbert Vault Company's survey of funeral attitudes and trends, almost 80 percent of the respondents indicated preference for a traditional burial. Only 14.4 percent indicated an interest in cremation.

Attitudes toward cremation differ greatly according to the region of the country. In the East/South Central states only 2.6 percent of the population showed a preference for cremation. In the Pacific states 31.2 percent of the people selected it.

The more highly educated are more likely to choose cremation. Those with post-graduate degrees selected it at 30.9 percent. Those with only a grammar school education selected it at 4.2 percent.

One thing which may hurt the cremation business is the lack of candor. Their eagerness to sell urns, burial plots, and columbarium space may frighten off the economy-minded. Some of their literature is definitely prejudiced against scattering, keeping the remains, or burying them on personal property. All three are legal in most areas.

The interest in cremation is at present steady and growing. *Reader's Digest* has published at least three articles on the subject. Each has resulted in thousands of letters from people requesting copies.

In San Diego a special no-frills cremation is made available for $250, roughly the amount of the Social Security benefit. These services, called Telophase, are short and simple. The body is wrapped in a plastic shroud and refrigerated. As soon as the paperwork is completed, it is taken directly to a crematory. The remains are then scattered at sea by a Navy chaplain.

In some areas of the country burial co-ops have existed for a number of years. Their total effect to date has probably been minimal. They have been tried in Minnesota for fifty years and are dwindling in numbers. At one time the state had thirty co-ops. It now has ten. Three thousand members make up the Minnesota Valley Burial Association.

Ideally they save the members $300 to $500 on a funeral. The individual then receives 20 percent of the co-op's annual profits in return. Funeral directors say that co-ops have negligible effect on the funeral business.

The St. Francis Burial Society in Washington, D.C., is attempting innovative approaches to funeral arrangements.

Their magazine, *Quarterly,* publishes hints on how to do many of the jobs connected with funerals. They tell the family how to remove the body from the hospital, wash it, dress it, and obtain a pine box. The family is instructed also in how to file a death certificate and how to get the burial or cremation certificate.

This society makes pine boxes available to help beat high costs.

As we have suggested, some funeral directors work with cooperatives and societies, but most are unimpressed. Charles Kates, Editor of *American Funeral Director,* protested the prices being charged by the Lutheran Burial Association of Chicago. Through that association the church which holds the funeral service receives $150, according to the magazine. This represents a sizable contribution to a nonprofit organization. There is also a charge for "administrative costs" and a charitable gift. It appears that there is money to be made even in this arrangement.

The future seems also to hold an increased emphasis on donations of organs. As transplants become more popular the public is becoming more aware of their value. Cards are being made available by several organizations to make it easier to contribute.

In the state where I live, donor cards are now given to everyone when they receive their driver's license. The individual can fill out the card and have two witnesses sign it. One can designate which organs he wants to donate, or whether he will give his entire body.

This is another area where funeral directors shine. Most of them can qualify to remove the cornea from an eye and greatly increase the possibility of its use. Their eagerness to do this is a compassionate service which greatly helps their public relations.

The process is called eye enucleation. In the state of New Jersey 250 funeral directors have taken a course to perform this procedure. In one year the directors removed 340 cornea. Of these 140 went for transplants while the other 200 were used in research.

A funeral director plays a vital role because of the time involved and the necessity of removing a cornea within five hours after death. The director of the New Jersey Eye Institute reports that since the morticians became involved in the program they have not missed receiving one pair of donated eyes.

It would appear that in the future fewer transplantable organs will be buried. This is especially true as the population becomes convinced of the uselessness of burying them.

The donating of entire bodies to anatomical use may be another matter. A large push is being made to educate the public concerning the need for cadavers for study and research. It remains to be seen whether the effort will produce a sizable trend in this direction.

Merely donating a body does not guarantee that it will be accepted. Under certain conditions the body may be rejected despite the clear intentions of the deceased. If the person dies from certain causes the body may be turned down. It is best to check with a local medical school before your family depends on acceptance of a donation.

No payment is made for cadavers. After the research has been completed, the body is given a dignified funeral service at no expense to the family. No one should do this without first being satisfied with the agreement.

Anyone who plans to leave his body to medical research would be wise to contact the institution involved. Check out the procedure for yourself. The National Funeral Directors Association believes it is reasonable to expect help from a local funeral director.

In Los Angeles someone began a unique service. He writes eulogies for people who want a "different" funeral. His clientele consist mostly of those who have untraditional religious ties. He charges $75 for each eulogy and often adds interesting side attractions. During one service two Great Danes stood beside the casket. At another funeral a tap dancer performed a final tribute. It is unclear whether such unconventional service will sweep the country. So far the innovator writes for five customers a week and is hoping to expand his business. He reports good cooperation from the funeral directors.

Almost as unusual is the widely reported funeral of a Hemingford, Nebraska, farmer. William Meinke, age eighty, offered to pay $500 to the high school band if they would march in his funeral procession. The forty-five members accepted the offer and marched the two miles from the Methodist church to the local cemetery. One hundred relatives and friends joined the entourage for the forty-minute trip.

That was not the first time a funeral has included a marching band. Presidents and other world figures regularly have bands march in the processions. In Dixieland, New Orleans jazz bands still accompany the funerals of noted musicians. During the procession for Louis Cottrell the band played "Oh, Didn't He Ramble" while his mourners danced.

Funeral practices are sometimes dictated by current fads. Possibly in the future there will be another wave of interest in freezing bodies. Several groups have promoted this, offering the prospect of bringing the deceased back to life after science has become more sophisticated.

And don't be too surprised if tomorrow's funeral arrangements are made at your local department store. You might charge it on your credit card the same way you purchase lawn furniture. A famous department store in England has started this streamlined service.

TWELVE
JESUS CHRIST
AND FLOWERS

People spend a great deal of money on funerals. If we aimed to bury our deceased as cheaply as possible, drastic cuts could be made. But in our thirst for economy, we need to be careful we don't become ridiculous.

It sounds noble, practical, even righteous to tell the public, "Please omit flowers"; but stop and think carefully. Do we really want to eliminate all expressions of love and affection? Is it truly Christian to strip life to the bare and cold?

Most of us passionately hate getting ripped off. We feel that certain special occasions are being rammed down our throats. Commercial interests are pushing their products, and frankly, we resent it. But let's not throw out the diamonds and the dirt together.

Some actions are loving and considerate, yet they have no utilitarian value. A box of candy probably does few wives any good; yet the thought is almost worth gold. We don't take our children to an amusement park to educate them; it is just a kind and giving thing to do. When was the last time we took our family to a restaurant just to save money?

After reading this chapter you may still want to omit flowers. Possibly that is the best practice for some. But all of us should consider the wider picture first. Are we prepared to become bone-bare utilitarian? What is the long-range effect of this attitude? Did Jesus practice it? Is there solid Christian teaching to support it? These are questions worth everyone's consideration.

Who can appreciate funeral flowers? Certainly the deceased can't. However, this doesn't settle the question. A dad, mother, husband, wife, or child wants to say "I love you" to someone who has died, or to a survivor. How? He or she could stand by the coffin and say it silently. Or he might read a poem or go off alone and play the flute. All these expressions are legitimate because love is not utilitarian.

Another person wants to pick a bunch of flowers from a field. Someone else orders a spray from the local florist. Is one of these expressions better than the other? By no means. But one could be a personal preference. It also might be more convenient. To me it seems shaky to say, "It is wrong to spend money to say 'I love you.'" We do it all the time and people have done so for centuries.

An individual sits in his living room in a $200 overstuffed chair. He is watching his $500 color television set with a $25 book in his hand. He leans toward his wife and says, "Let's give $15 to the Community Chest in Aunt Agnes' name. Flowers are just a waste."

It is difficult to define waste. If we choose to be purely practical, our lives would change immediately. How many things are unnecessary? Hot dog warmers, hamburger grills, slippers, watermelon ballers. But we still collect and use them.

Someone dies and it becomes a waste to say we loved him. A mother loses her eight-year-old boy and we try to persuade her to be practical. "Don't put flowers on his coffin, it would only be a waste." Is there anything Christian about this attitude?

In the New Testament there is an excellent example to consult. Jesus Christ taught something about expressions of love and waste. The story is found in John 12, where a dinner was being given in Jesus' honor in Bethany. His hostesses were Mary and Martha. Lazarus was there, having been recently raised from the dead.

When they were reclining at the table Mary did a terribly impractical thing. She opened a jar of expensive perfume and poured it on Jesus' feet. The fragrance was so strong it filled the entire house.

The perfume was nard, a substance extracted from plants. How expensive was this luxury? It is hard to compare first-century denarii with American dollars. We do know it would have taken the average working person one full year to earn the 300 denarii necessary to buy this perfume. How much would it cost today?

Mary simply poured it on Jesus' feet and it was gone. She then wiped his feet with her hair. Since Jesus and his disciples were taking collections from crowds as they traveled from town to town, how could he sit still for this terrible waste?

If this puzzles us, it startled Judas first. He raised the logical utilitarian objection: "Why wasn't the perfume sold? We could have given the money to the poor" (v. 5).

Frankly, Judas had a good point. Israel, despite its generosity, was burdened with poor people. The streets of Jerusalem were haunted with beggars and drifters. Unemployment was a harsh reality and gangs roamed the streets with nothing to do but cause trouble. Palestine was not without its social problems. Yet Jesus sat still while a year's wages were poured on the ground. How could he justify his behavior?

For explanation's sake, we understand Judas' problem. John, the author, tells us what the desperado really wanted. Judas was serving as treasurer for the disciples. Later he would steal the money.

But Jesus is a little more difficult to understand. He insisted that Judas back off and leave Mary alone. She had every right to express her love if she wanted to. And if the method was too impractical for Judas, he would have to stew. Jesus was confident that Mary had done the loving, sane thing.

Christ insists it would have been proper for Mary to use this perfume at his burial. It would have been all right if she had poured 300 denarii on his lifeless body. He did not consider it pagan or wasteful but rather a loving act.

Normally a body in Palestine was packed with spices and perfumes. As the cadaver decayed, some of the stench was offset by additives. While unnecessary, such preservation was a loving action.

Mary would have no chance to express her love in this way after the removal of Jesus' body from the cross. Joseph and Nicodemus would be fortunate if they could get the body at all. Consequently, Jesus is telling his friends, in essence, "Thank you for being so thoughtful and doing it now." Later, when he was all alone, memories like this may have helped him.

If the story seems odd up to this point, the next statement is just as amazing. Jesus tells Judas and the disciples, "You will always have the poor with you." What type of callous statement is this? Jesus had gained a following among the poor. Was he now expressing contempt for the whole lot?

No. Rather he was holding life in its proper perspective. There are people who need help. Millions are starving, ill-housed, uneducated, dying. Certainly they need the warm arm of caring Christians. But Christ calls us back to reality. A balanced life not only helps the poor but also cares for personal needs. The expressing of love and the comforting of relatives are part of the balanced life.

Normally we don't give away all we have. There are exceptions and the apostle Barnabas was one of them (Acts 4:36, 37). The rest of us purchase clothing, food, an automobile, and *TV Guide*.

For instance, a couple reach their fifteenth wedding anniversary, and the husband decides to take his beautiful woman out to dinner. Then feelings of guilt flood the pair. How can they waste money in a restaurant when so many are starving? They decide to exercise their Christian austerity and stay home. The next day they mail a check to their favorite mission.

The principle may seem sound, but I think Jesus Christ stops to differ. The poor will be there tomorrow and the next day. Tonight, take your special pair of brown eyes to dinner. Invest some time, energy, and money into the person you have loved all these years. The poor will still be here later and you will help them.

Jesus took a considerable risk in teaching us this. He left himself wide open for misinterpretation. But he was a firm believer in the balanced life, and he practiced it. The Galilean was criticized for not being austere enough (Matthew 11:19); yet he refused to be frightened into the dank dungeon of total deprivation.

It's easy to distort the Christian life. For some, every comfort and dollar spent on ourselves is an embarrassment. Some feel guilt at every turn, and when death enters our family we are often overwhelmed by guilt. We should not allow such guilt to disfigure our perspective. It's no sin to express our love. We say "I love you" while our loved ones are alive. We can also say it after they die.

The flower industry is not paying me to have this written. How they may feel about this point is unimportant. The principle is tremendously significant. Possibly giving flowers is not the way you want to express your love. Excellent. You may want instead to write a poem and print it in the paper or frame it on your wall. You can fold it into the deceased's favorite book. By whatever means you say "I love you," you need not feel guilty about it.

If this doesn't appeal to you, maybe music does. Stand beside the coffin some time and sing or play a song with special meaning. Let the love flow. The way you choose to let it pour out is entirely up to you.

It could be that a memorial fund is the best way to let it flow. You are grateful to the Cancer Society and their efforts. If your money will help bring a cure closer, it is worth a try. Maybe the Gideons were near to your relative's heart. The writing of a check could be a highly compassionate thing to do. But don't feel trapped as if such giving is the only Christian avenue to follow. Some charitable organizations may be preying on our guilt rather than accepting expressions of our love.

A person goes through life with financial pleas bombarding him. The Scouts, the school band, the hospital auxiliary, the church bell tower, orphans, boys club—an endless array. They are probably all good causes. We give a little bit here and maybe a bit more there.

In some cases memorial funds are preying on our guilt. After all, the person is dead. He can't appreciate what you do. Why not be Christian and practical? Giving to a worthy cause makes a lot more sense. At this point Jesus butts in to remind us of something: that it doesn't have to "make sense." This is why he objected to Judas. The disciple's argument was utilitarian. Christ was warm and compassionate.

Naturally our options are open. We need to come to believe this. We are not boxed in to a couple of socially accepted practices. How would you like to do it? The best way is to think about it and discuss the subject with relatives and friends. Then the funerals we plan will express our feelings and personalities.

This approach is not without problems. Jesus was still alive when the perfume was poured out. Maybe the example teaches us to give to the living rather than the dead. This is a good observation, but it doesn't quite solve the problem.

Christ told Judas it was fine for Mary to save this perfume for his burial. It would have been fine if she had used it on him after he died. The import of Jesus' remark is not "I'm glad she used it while I am still alive." She could have poured it either before or after his death and still had his approval.

Later it would be difficult to administer the perfume. Joseph of Arimathea and Nicodemus undertook the burial at considerable personal risk.

Mary Magdalene, Mary the mother of James, and Salome all went to the tomb after the burial. Their intention was to complete the anointing of the body. Since Jesus was gone, the final preparation was impossible (Mark 15:47—16:1).

Jesus was definitely putting out the green light for posthumous expressions. He had no quarrel with people who wanted to put love into concrete form.

Henry Jacobson, a Scripture Press editor, has publicly requested the absence of flowers. He is an excellent Bible student and doubtless knows this passage well (John 12). His logic is solid. Mrs. Jacobson is allergic to flowers, and besides, they fade quickly. He would rather his friends gave contributions to the President's Fund at Wheaton College.

This is an excellent decision and hopefully his relatives and associates will comply. The only danger is in believing that such action is *the* Christian thing to do. There is danger in becoming totally practical. (Once more with feeling.) There is danger in becoming totally practical!

For some survivors flowers are the most meaningful expression. They read the cards and think of the people who sent them. It is not a forced acceptance but genuine appreciation for thoughtfulness.

Sooner or later someone must raise a valid objection to florists. There are people in the flower business who are greedy and tasteless. Can there be any doubt about it? Florists are people. Some are kind and caring; others are pushy and unscrupulous. They are much like the general population. There is no need to malign them all because of those who have wrong motives.

To balance the picture we have to remember that the memorial fund business is not always the New Jerusalem. Some among their number also know how to milk the most from tears. More than one charitable organization has been cruel in its collection methods and fraudulent in its expenditures.

When someone dies, unscrupulous solicitors for a memorial fund may act quickly. They set up a special project in honor of the deceased and begin to collect from the friends. All for a good cause, naturally. But they have set up the project without the knowledge or consent of the family. They are simply taking advantage of a family's grief. All we have in organizations is people, and people are likely to do anything. The righteousness of their cause does not guarantee their character.

Jesus Christ knew he was going to die under unusual circumstances. There would be violence and separation from the people he loved. After the crucifixion both the old and new friends responded in compassion. Nicodemus and Joseph came forward with expensive spices and perfumes to prepare the body.

To complete the preparation of Christ's body they used seventy-five pounds of myrrh and aloes. The myrrh was a powdered form of the same perfume mentioned in John 12. It was made of aromatic gum resin. The Egyptians used it extensively in their burials.

Aloe was a powdered wood. It was priced high because of its pleasant odor which increases as the wood decays. To bring so much of the two was unusual. The body preparation was more suited for a king than for a carpenter-prophet. But this funeral, from the tomb on, was an expensive affair. Nicodemus and Joseph were evidently spending from their own pockets.

The concepts of austerity had not penetrated this team. In open conscience and serious devotion they expressed their love in a tangible, and if you will, wasted way. But it was something they wanted to do.

Faced with the grief of death we need to be encouraged to feel free in expressing our love. There are two tragic extremes to avoid. One, don't believe that we show our love by the extravagance of our spending. Two, don't believe that we show our piety by our frugality.

THIRTEEN
THE MARTIN
HAUSERS

It is the type of thing that happens every once in a while. A pastor doesn't get too excited about it. Someone in the congregation asks the minister to pay a call on a family. I try to avoid most of these situations because I feel unwelcome when I am not sure the family wants a visit.

The Hausers' house was a small white frame structure. The last person you would expect to answer the door was a maid. But there she was with neat white apron and a broom in hand. After I introduced myself she stepped to one side, and behind her stood Mrs. Ida Hauser, a gray-haired woman in her seventies with a marked German accent. The furniture in the living room was inexpensive and old. The maid was a cleaning lady lent by a local charity organization.

In the adjoining dining room my eye was caught by a hospital bed flanked by two or three large oxygen shells. The bed was occupied by a frail man, Martin Hauser. Mr. Hauser had suffered, I think, five heart attacks, and for some years he had been weak. Mrs. Hauser had cancer, but she was trying to avoid treatment until her husband was stronger.

We all three talked for a while. About his health, about Christ, about food, and about who was helping them. We got to know each other. Our church arranged to send some things to them at Christmas.

After the first of the year, while I was out of town, Martin Hauser grew still weaker and was hospitalized. There was no hope for him. As the good German doctor put it, "Only God is keeping him alive now." The family gathered around and for hours waited and watched.

Mr. Hauser would revive, talk clearly, and then retreat again into semiconsciousness. During the times I sat by his bed he and I would talk about what Christ meant to him. He told me about his confirmation in the Lutheran Church in Germany. I asked him if he had placed his personal faith in Christ at that time. His head lifted. In that drawn and tired face, his eyes lit up and glittered like the sparkle on a young lover's face. "Oh, yes!" he said, "and when I accepted him the pastor said to me . . . Oh, I can still hear it in German, but I can't say it in English."

In the hours that we spent alone we talked about heaven and whether he was ready to go there, and he remarked, "Yes, I am ready to go. It is only the suffering and dragging it out that makes it so bad."

Someone watching such a scene learns a great deal. I think of Mrs. Hauser standing by the bed, feeding him, fighting off the decay in her own body. She knew he would not live, but as she put it, "If only he could get strong enough to come home so I could take care of him when he dies."

At night a young pastor leaves the hospital with renewed appreciation for his own family. A pastor is a richer man because he has to visit so many patients. He is constantly reminded of how frail his loved ones are. All Mrs. Hauser wanted was the opportunity to bring her husband home one more time. Yet my family was healthy at home, while I took them for granted.

The Hausers were amazing in their love and sacrifice. Like many other German-Americans, they had close relatives in Germany during the war. Martin Hauser worked two jobs in those days—one to support his family and the second so he could send food overseas to others whom he loved. After the war he felt rewarded by knowing that many times the only food his German relatives had was what he so faithfully and lovingly sacrificed to send.

After Martin Hauser's funeral Mrs. Hauser became confined to bed now and again, as she took cobalt treatments. She knew the treatments were fruitless, but her spirits remained high. She was genuinely grateful that she had maintained her strength to help her husband to the end.

She taught me another lesson which I am sure she didn't realize. One day she said, "Thank God for Medicare. If it were not for Medicare we would have lost our little home and everything."

I was one of those old cynics who always knocked the government and treated it like a meddlesome old fool. I thought it had no business offering Social Security. Let people take care of themselves. Yet if the Hausers had been forced to look to local churches in their financial disaster, they would have been hopelessly ruined. The churches will not usually take the responsibility, so thank God for some kind of government assistance.

The last time I visited Mrs. Hauser she was only semiconscious, and the visit was brief. The next day she was dead.

I remember the funeral service in a beautiful chapel at the funeral home. I had prepared a message on the twenty-third Psalm in which I discussed how Mrs. Hauser could have written it as well as David. She, too, had walked through the valley of death twice—once three months earlier, with her husband, and now on her own.

When I finished I sat down behind the podium and people started to file past the casket. I didn't want to cry, and I fought the feeling; but it had to come. I sat there and wept tears of real sorrow and separation.

The Hausers had never entered the walls of our small church. When I met them it was too late for that. But those two people whom someone asked me to visit have left a mark on me that can never be removed. I hope each pastor will meet a family like this one—early in his ministry.

Personally I've never conducted an easy funeral. If granddad was ninety-nine and had contracted sixteen diseases it was still a hard time to go through. There were people left behind. There was a vicious ripping asunder of lives. Any way you sliced it, it was a painful experience for someone. If a pastor has many funerals, he has to learn to insulate himself. After all, he can't bear burying his best friend every few weeks. For a pastor, it isn't at all uncommon to be sitting in a side room telling an Irish joke with the funeral director or swapping old baseball stories, and then jumping up a few minutes later to assume a fairly somber face and read a verse in the Psalms.

Funerals and money are pretty touchy subjects, and every once in a while some crusader takes a few swings at the clergy and morticians. Let the undertakers defend themselves, but the clergy are really in an awkward fix.

Some feel that ministers should not receive money for conducting funerals. For several years I myself felt the same way. I tried returning the money, but that often led to a hassle or a misunderstanding. Then I came up with a clever scheme which seemed to comfort my conscience. We had developed a scholarship fund in our church for young people who were entering a vocation of the ministry. Here was my chance. I would now put all funeral money into the fund and then write an extremely pious letter to the bereaved, announcing my mammoth benevolence.

After some years of playing this game of righteous hide-and-seek, I was cured by a gentleman of about sixty. He had lost his wife suddenly, and after the funeral he gave me a generous check. During the dinner which followed the funeral, I sauntered up to the husband and in holy tones said, "Thanks for the generous check, but of course I will give the money to some worthy cause." That man looked at me squarely and with tears in his eyes said firmly, "If I'd wanted someone else to have the money I would have given it to someone else."

Forget it! Count me out! From now on no more struggle, ups, downs, or schemes. If a person does not want to pay me, fine; let him keep it. If another wants to pay me, fine, I'll take it.

That policy is adequate for church attenders, but what about those whom you do not know at all? A funeral director calls and asks a minister whether he is available for a family who has not been attending any place. I see nothing wrong with the family paying for this type of service, though many ministers do return the honorarium, especially from needy families.

This latter type of funeral is usually of good interest to a minister. Here is a family with a genuine need, confronting the reality of death, with no church home. They may be quite confused about God. It is generally a good experience to sit with them and discuss the promises of Jesus Christ. Sometimes relatives are bitter at God because of the death, but other times they simply want to know.

Once in a while you will meet a pastor who is exceptionally good at getting this type of family into church. One such was Rev. Andrew Walker. A certain Catholic funeral director just loved Pastor Walker. Back in those days many priests were reluctant to officiate at anyone's funeral unless they knew something about the deceased. This one funeral director would just throw a fit when a priest refused to come or balked at going to the cemetery, leaving the director to give the committal.

Consequently, he was always eager to call Pastor Walker, who without the slightest flinch would run right over and greet the family like long-lost cousins from Newark. After the graveside service Walker would level with the family like a football coach.

"I know your background isn't the same as that of our church, but I don't care. You need a pastor and a church, and I'll be looking for you this Sunday. OK?"

And often on Sundays such people would be there, smiling and meeting people as if they were charter members. Sheep stealer? More power to him. If people are not involved in a local church, they are game for anyone who can help them know Christ better.

Most of my own "unchurched" funerals were good experiences. Only once did I hit a sour note, and it may have been my fault. I went to the funeral home to meet a man in his middle forties to make the final arrangements for his mother's service. We sat and talked and I tried to gear the conversation to his mother while offering some comfort in Christ. The gentleman obviously couldn't care less about what I was saying, and he drew out a list of all of his mother's accomplishments (which were considerable) and asked me if I would explain to those in attendance what a good woman his mother was.

Doubtless his mother was wonderful, but I didn't know her and felt awfully funny being asked to canonize her before the group. I explained my reservations and he gave me a classic disgusted look.

Maybe I was young, cruel, and feeling a little haughty.

Though funerals are sad affairs, ministers seem to survive them with reasonable composure. The closest I ever came to a crying spell during a service was for Mrs. Hauser, but at one other time I must confess I didn't make it dry-eyed.

While I was pastoring one church two women from the congregation crashed on a country road and both were killed instantly. Their funerals were scheduled back to back on Friday and Saturday, and the church was packed both days.

The first service was for the older woman. That night I intentionally went to bed early to avoid getting weak. The second service progressed smoothly, and I came to the end of the twelve-minute message. There was only one short sentence left to be said: "We will meet again." As I stood there and tried to say it, the tears started to roll and I couldn't talk. With her children and husband seated close in front of me, I fought and fought—and then finally said the four words.

At the time I felt bad about not being able to hold out to the end, but as I look back my grief seems to have been only natural.

FOURTEEN
GETTING READY
FOR A FUNERAL

This is a big order. How does a person get ready to cope with death? Fortunately there are a few simple guidelines which help ease the pain. None of the steps are profound or earthshaking. Sometimes we miss them because they are too obvious.

Far and away the best preparation for tomorrow's funeral is to have a good day today. The basic ingredients which make the present beautiful are the same qualities necessary to a bearable funeral. Peace, fulfillment, forgiveness, a healthy humor, a reaching out to handle the good things in life—these are lasting values. To know you have extended yourself to others and brightened their day. Acts of love do not make the parting harder. Rather, they ease the pain.

Peace with God is a prime example. Christians by the carload seem worried about meeting God. Even though they are redeemed in Christ they are afraid of death. They act as if God is going to get them on the other side. That attitude makes a miserable existence. Continually they worry about judgment.

Because of this, many Christians face death with the same fear as the nonbeliever. They concentrate on uncertainty, chastisement, and the supposed vengefulness of God.

Throw it away! Live today with Christ and tomorrow will

take care of itself. Accept his patience, love, and forgiveness. If we lean easily into the grace of Jesus Christ we have nothing to fear in death.

If the purpose of life were to prepare for death, the job would be too great. Death is too large, too final, too painful to handle. But if we can cope with today, Christ will take care of tomorrow. With good reason Jesus said, "Therefore do not be anxious about tomorrow, for tomorrow will be anxious for itself. Let the day's own trouble be sufficient for the day." (Matthew 6:34, RSV).

Since it makes sense to keep short accounts with God, it makes as much sense to keep close to people. Some of us are prone to sulk for days over the least nonsense. Life is too brief for us to take time out to suck our thumbs. Your spouse may have let you down, but the next move is up to you. Do you want to intensify the problem by dragging it out? Would you rather heal a wound or pick at it to keep it bleeding?

Death is difficult enough to grapple with without a host of ghosts hovering. These spooks are the acid-tipped darts we ourselves have thrown too often. At a funeral this acid has a way of burning doubly.

Authorities on human behavior tell us that a person's most traumatic experience is losing his spouse. Many cannot survive the shock. Often a surviving husband or wife is dead within a couple of years after this tragedy. It would be foolish to add to the pain by unnecessary wounds. How much better to feel, like Paul, "I thank God upon every remembrance of you" (Philippians 1:3).

A hospital chaplain made a strange observation about human nature. He feels that those with a healthy sense of humor are the ones who face death the best. There may be some support for what he says.

Consider two types of people. The first looks back at years of disappointments, broken dreams, and bitterness. Death is to him merely one more in a long string of horrors. Then look at the person who hung loose and learned to laugh. He remembers dancing eyes and a smile like a new hubcap. Death is painful to both persons, but it may be a little easier for the one who learned to laugh. A wise man said, "A cheerful heart does good like medicine, but a broken spirit makes one sick" (Proverbs 17:22, TLB).

The best investment in death preparation is to put the most into life today. This doesn't mean wild abandonment. A good day doesn't imply that we ignore death. Death doesn't go away. Certain decisions need to be made. But having considered it carefully, we don't dwell on the subject. We move on to plant and harvest the fruits of living.

Part of the time that we spend in education should focus on death. Somewhere among the courses in astrology, palm reading, and squirrel mounting, there should be room for one on death and funerals.

If no one else can, certainly churches could offer a helpful class once every couple of years. The Christian church is in a position to speak with authority. It can discuss cremation, body donations, transplants, and the questions of preservation. There is no better institution to give direction on guilt than the one which heralds Jesus Christ.

Our inability to handle death is seen in the tragic results which follow. We have already mentioned the trauma faced by losing a spouse. A similar emotional disaster occurs when a family loses a child. After such a bereavement some parents are unable to resolve their feelings, and some marriages even crumble in divorce. The church which addresses itself to death and funerals could de-fuse many of these situations.

Death is a natural function of life. It's not like robbery or riots, self-imposed by man. The minute a man is born he is marked as mortal. Some literature is being published which merely compares man with the rest of nature. Grass dies, bugs are eaten, elephants are vulnerable. Man is then listed as merely one more part of nature's giant scheme.

This concept is only half the loaf. Man is also immortal. Believers need to teach the second half as well.

There are many small groups in our Christian circles. Church groups, Bible study groups, growth groups, home coffee groups. Part of their contribution can be a willingness to discuss the funerals which face us all. Such discussions can air our fears as well as our faith. Fear has a way of dissipating in the sunshine. Fears are like night crawlers—they prefer the dark and dank.

After we have read about funerals and discussed them, we might want to visit a funeral home. Go as a group. Ask questions and compare notes. Talk also with cemetery managers, operators of crematories, or memorial society officers. Different members can gather comparative prices. The entire venture can be educational, exciting, and satisfying.

After all this activity, we can then leave the subject. The matter of funerals should be visited occasionally but never dwelt on. The best preparation for death is life. How simple can anything be? We cannot afford to spend our life dying or fencing with its fears.

Then someday as believers in Jesus Christ we will lay down our burdens. We will also put down our sundaes, our fishing rods, our race cars, our golf clubs, our garden rakes. Quickly we will enter into new pleasures in the satisfying corridors of eternity.

"For I am in a strait betwixt two, having a desire to depart, and to be with Christ, which is far better" (Philippians 1:23).

CHOICES AND NOTES

Too few of us make decisions about our own funerals. Consequently, most families are left to guess how the deceased wanted his final services. How often have ministers visited with grieving relatives who were agonized over choices? "Would Aunt Agnes have liked a pink interior?" "This cold metal doesn't really fit Allen's personality."

We can help our survivors by letting our preferences be known in advance. Not that we want to lock our relatives in. Knowing that times and practices change, we want to give them enough freedom to alter our requests. But because funerals are for the living, and we want to make their decisions easier, we also aim to express enough of our personal choices.

Naturally this atitude eliminates anything too shocking or bizarre. We don't want the Empire State Building lifted so we can be buried under it. We won't ask to be buried in a 1957 Chevy. We are trying to make it easy, not difficult.

A good approach is to discuss the following pages of this book with our relatives. Make sure they understand and are not surprised later. Visit a funeral home, write some letters, gather dependable information, then make some intelligent decisions.

After you have filled in these pages, be sure they aren't hidden away. At the time it is most needed, the volume may be impossible to find. This is the reason we should not leave funeral instructions in a will or in a safe deposit box. It is probable that neither the will nor the deposit box will be accessible until after the funeral is complete. Some will want to leave a set of instructions with the minister.

While you fill in these pages, enjoy yourself. You are doing a mature thing by facing reality. You can go on living a full life because you have prepared for the eventual day.

A. This is how I feel about my burial.
   My *first* preferences are:
   1. Funeral Home:

   2. Casket:

   3. Viewing and open casket:

   4. Vaults and concrete containers:

B. This is how I feel about cremation:

Disposal of my cremains:

C. This is how I feel about donating my organs.

I have filled out a donor card and this is where you can find it:

D. This is how I feel about donating my entire body to a medical institution.

I have filled out a card and this is where you can find it:

E. This is my opinion about flowers at my funeral.

F. This is how I feel about giving to a memorial fund instead of sending flowers.

    The charity I want to select for a memorial fund is:

G. My first preference for a cemetery is:

H. This is how I feel about a headstone.

I. If the doctor requests an autopsy:

J. Do I want a church funeral?

K. My first selections for music are:

L. If they are available I would choose these pallbearers:

M. Any organizations I want to participate in my funeral service:

N. I particularly want this to be part of my final service:

O. These are the Scriptures I most want read at my funeral service:

P. I would also like to have this read:

Q. My *first* preference for a participating clergyman would be:

R. These are the financial arrangements I have made for my funeral.

Insurance policy:

Cemetery plot:

Pre-paid funeral:

Where documents for these or other arrangements can be found:

S. This is how I feel about leaving this life and meeting God.

T. In general this is how I feel about my eventual funeral.

U. These are a few thoughts I would like to leave with my relatives and friends.

SELECTING BIBLE PASSAGES

Many people have a favorite passage of Scripture they would like read at their funeral. Here are some of the more familiar ones to choose from.

PSALM 23

The Lord is my shepherd; I shall not want.

He maketh me to lie down in green pastures: he leadeth me beside the still waters.

He restoreth my soul: he leadeth me in the paths of righteousness for his name's sake.

Yea, though I walk through the valley of the shadow of death, I will fear no evil: for thou art with me; thy rod and thy staff they comfort me.

Thou preparest a table before me in the presence of mine enemies: thou anointest my head with oil; my cup runneth over.

Surely goodness and mercy shall follow me all the days of my life: and I will dwell in the house of the Lord for ever.

King James Version

1 THESSALONIANS 4:13-18

And now, dear brothers, I want you to know what happens to a Christian when he dies so that when it happens, you will not be full of sorrow, as those are who have no hope. For since we believe that Jesus died and then came back to life again, we can also believe that when Jesus returns, God will bring back with him all the Christians who have died.

I can tell you this directly from the Lord: that we who are still living when the Lord returns will not rise to meet him ahead of those who are in their graves. For the Lord himself will come down from heaven with a mighty shout and with the soul-stirring cry of the archangel and the great trumpet-call of God. And the believers who are dead will be the first to rise to meet the Lord. Then we who are still alive and remain on the earth will be caught up with them in the clouds to meet the Lord in the air and remain with him forever. So comfort and encourage each other with this news.

The Living Bible

1 CORINTHIANS 15:50-57

I declare to you, brothers, that flesh and blood cannot inherit the kingdom of God, nor does the perishable inherit the imperishable. Listen, I tell you a mystery: We shall not all sleep, but we shall all be changed—in a flash, in the twinkling of an eye, at the last trumpet. For the trumpet will sound, the dead will be raised imperishable, and we shall be changed. For the perishable must clothe itself with the imperishable, and the mortal with immortality. When the perishable has been clothed with the imperishable, and the mortal with immortality, then the saying that is written will come true: "Death has been swallowed up in victory."

"Where, O death, is your victory?

Where, O death, is your sting?"

The sting of death is sin, and the power of sin is the law. But thanks be to God! He gives us the victory through our Lord Jesus Christ.

New International Version

HEBREWS 11:8-13

By faith Abraham, when he was called to go out into a place which he should after receive for an inheritance, obeyed; and he went out, not knowing whither he went.

By faith he sojourned in the land of promise, as in a strange country, dwelling in tabernacles with Isaac and Jacob, the heirs with him of the same promise: For he looked for a city which hath foundations, whose builder and maker is God.

Through faith also Sara herself received strength to conceive seed, and was delivered of a child when she was past age, because she judged him faithful who had promised.

Therefore sprang there even of one, and him as good as dead, so many as the stars of the sky in multitude, and as the sand which is by the sea shore innumerable.

These all died in faith, not having received the promises, but having seen them afar off, and were persuaded of them, and embraced them, and confessed that they were strangers and pilgrims on the earth.

King James Version

PSALM 91:1-12

We live within the shadow of the Almighty, sheltered by the God who is above all gods.

This I declare, that he alone is my refuge, my place of safety; he is my God, and I am trusting him. For he rescues you from every trap, and protects you from the fatal plague. He will shield you with his wings! They will shelter you. His faithful promises are your armor. Now you don't need to be afraid of the dark any more, nor fear the dangers of the day; nor dread the plagues of darkness, nor disasters in the morning.

Though a thousand fall at my side, though ten thousand are dying around me, the evil will not touch me. I will see how the wicked are punished but I will not share it. For Jehovah is my refuge! I choose the God above all gods to shelter me. How then can evil overtake me or any plague come near? For he orders his angels to protect you wherever you go. They will steady you with their hands to keep you from stumbling against the rocks on the trail.

The Living Bible

REVELATION 21:1-4

Then I saw a new heaven and a new earth, for the first heaven and the first earth had passed away, and there was no longer any sea. I saw the Holy City, the new Jerusalem, coming down out of heaven from God, prepared as a bride beautifully dressed for her husband. And I heard a loud voice from the throne saying, "Now the dwelling of God is with men, and he will live with them. They will be his people, and God himself will be with them and be their God. He will wipe every tear from their eyes. There will be no more death or mourning or crying or pain, for the old order of things has passed away."

New International Version

ECCLESIASTES 3:1-12

To every thing there is a season, and a time to every purpose under the heaven: a time to be born, and a time to die; a time to plant, and a time to pluck up that which is planted; a time to kill, and a time to heal; a time to break down, and a time to build up; a time to weep, and a time to laugh; a time to mourn, and a time to dance; a time to cast away stones, and a time to gather stones together; a time to embrace, and a time to refrain from embracing; a time to get, and a time to lose; a time to keep, and a time to cast away; a time to rend, and a time to sew; a time to keep silence, and a time to speak; a time to love, and a time to hate; a time of war, and a time of peace.

What profit hath he that worketh in that wherein he laboureth?

I have seen the travail, which God hath given to the sons of men to be exercised in it.

He hath made everything beautiful in his time: also he hath set the world in their heart, so that no man can find out the work that God maketh from the beginning to the end.

I know that there is no good in them, but for a man to rejoice, and to do good in his life.

King James Version

JOHN 14:1-6

"Let not your heart be troubled. You are trusting God, now trust in me. There are many homes up there where my Father lives, and I am going to prepare them for your coming. When everything is ready, then I will come and get you, so that you can always be with me where I am. If this weren't so, I would tell you plainly. And you know where I am going and how to get there."

"No, we don't," Thomas said. "We haven't any idea where you are going, so how can we know the way?"

Jesus told him, "I am the Way—yes, and the Truth and the Life. No one can get to the Father except by means of me."

The Living Bible

2 TIMOTHY 4:6-8

For I am already being poured out as a drink offering, and the time has come for my departure. I have fought the good fight, I have finished the race, I have kept the faith. Now there is in store for me the crown of righteousness, which the Lord, the righteous Judge, will award to me on that day—and not only to me, but also to all who have longed for his appearing.

New International Version

PSALM 100

Make a joyful noise unto the Lord, all ye lands.

Serve the Lord with gladness; come before his presence with singing.

Know ye that the Lord he is God: it is he that hath made us, and not we ourselves; we are his people, and the sheep of his pasture.

Enter into his gates with thanksgiving, and into his courts with praise: be thankful unto him, and bless his name.

For the Lord is good; his mercy is everlasting; and his truth endureth to all generations.

King James Version

1 CORINTHIANS 13:11-13

It's like this: when I was a child I spoke and thought and reasoned as a child does. But when I became a man my thoughts grew far beyond those of my childhood, and now I have put away the childish things. In the same way, we can see and understand only a little about God now, as if we were peering at his reflection in a poor mirror; but someday we are going to see him in his completeness, face to face. Now all that I know is hazy and blurred, but then I will see everything clearly, just as clearly as God sees into my heart right now.

There are three things that remain—faith, hope, and love—and the greatest of these is love.

The Living Bible

PHILIPPIANS 1:19-23

For I know that through your prayers and the help given by the Spirit of Jesus Christ, what has happened to me will turn out for my deliverance. I eagerly expect and hope that I will in no way be ashamed, but will have sufficient courage so that now as always Christ will be exalted in my body, whether by life or by death. For to me, to live is Christ and to die is gain. If I am to go on living in the body, this will mean fruitful labor for me. Yet, what shall I choose? I do not know! I am torn between the two: I desire to depart and be with Christ, which is better by far.

New International Version

PHILIPPIANS 2:5-11

Let this mind be in you, which was also in Christ Jesus:

Who, being in the form of God, thought it not robbery to be equal with God: But made himself of no reputation, and took upon him the form of a servant, and was made in the likeness of men: And being found in fashion as a man, he humbled himself, and became obedient unto death, even the death of the cross.

Wherefore God also hath highly exalted him, and given him a name which is above every name: That at the name of Jesus every knee should bow, of things in heaven, and things in earth, and things under the earth; And that every tongue should confess that Jesus Christ is Lord, to the glory of God the Father.

King James Version

HEBREWS 9:24-27

For Christ has entered into heaven itself, to appear now before God as our Friend. It was not in the earthly place of worship that he did this, for that was merely a copy of the real temple in heaven. Nor has he offered himself again and again, as the high priest down here on earth offers animal blood in the Holy of Holies each year. If that had been necessary, then he would have had to die again and again, ever since the world began. But no! He came once for all, at the end of the age, to put away the power of sin forever by dying for us.

And . . . as it is destined that men die only once, and after that comes judgment.

The Living Bible

JOHN 11:17-27

On his arrival, Jesus found that Lazarus had already been in the tomb for four days. Bethany was less than two miles from Jerusalem, and many Jews had come to Martha and Mary to comfort them in the loss of their brother. When Martha heard that Jesus was coming, she went out to meet him, but Mary stayed at home.

"Lord," Martha said to Jesus, "if you had been here, my brother would not have died. But I know that even now God will give you whatever you ask."

Jesus said to her, "Your brother will rise again."

Martha answered, "I know he will rise again in the resurrection at the last day."

Jesus said to her, "I am the resurrection and the life. He who believes in me will live, even though he dies; and whoever lives and believes in me will never die. Do you believe this?"

"Yes, Lord," she told him, "I believe that you are the Christ, the Son of God, who was to come into the world."

New International Version

1 PETER 1:3-5

Blessed be the God and Father of our Lord Jesus Christ, which according to his abundant mercy hath begotten us again unto a lively hope by the resurrection of Jesus Christ from the dead,

To an inheritance incorruptible, and undefiled, and that fadeth not away, reserved in heaven for you,

Who are kept by the power of God through faith unto salvation ready to be revealed in the last time.

King James Version

2 CORINTHIANS 5:1-5

For we know that when this tent we live in now is taken down —when we die and leave these bodies—we will have wonderful new bodies in heaven, homes that will be ours forevermore, made for us by God himself, and not by human hands. How weary we grow of our present bodies. That is why we look forward eagerly to the day when we shall have heavenly bodies which we shall put on like new clothes. For we shall not be merely spirits without bodies. These earthly bodies make us groan and sigh, but we wouldn't like to think of dying and having no bodies at all. We want to slip into our new bodies so that these dying bodies will, as it were, be swallowed up by everlasting life. This is what God has prepared for us and, as a guarantee, he has given us his Holy Spirit.

The Living Bible

ROMANS 8:31-39

What, then, shall we say in response to this? If God is for us, who can be against us? He who did not spare his own Son, but gave him up for us all—how will he not also, along with him, graciously give us all things? Who will bring any charge against those whom God has chosen? It is God who justifies. Who is he that condemns? Christ Jesus, who died—more than that, who was raised to life—is at the right hand of God and is also interceding for us. Who shall separate us from the love of Christ? Shall trouble or hardship or persecution or famine or nakedness or danger or sword? As it is written:

"For your sake we face death all the day long;
we are considered as sheep to be slaughtered."

No, in all these things we are more than conquerors through him who loved us. For I am convinced that neither death nor life, neither angels nor demons, neither the present nor the future, nor any powers, neither height nor depth, nor anything else in all creation, will be able to separate us from the love of God that is in Christ Jesus our Lord.

New International Version

PSALM 1

Blessed is the man that walketh not in the counsel of the ungodly, nor standeth in the way of sinners, nor sitteth in the seat of the scornful.

But his delight is in the law of the Lord; and in his law doth he meditate day and night.

And he shall be like a tree planted by the rivers of water, that bringeth forth his fruit in his season; his leaf also shall not wither; and whatsoever he doeth shall prosper.

The ungodly are not so: but are like the chaff which the wind driveth away.

Therefore the ungodly shall not stand in the judgment, nor sinners in the congregation of the righteous.

For the Lord knoweth the way of the righteous: but the way of the ungodly shall perish.

King James Version

JOB 19:23-27

Oh, that I could write my plea with an iron pen in the rock forever.

But as for me, I know that my Redeemer lives, and that he will stand upon the earth at last. And I know that after this body has decayed, this body shall see God! Then he will be on my side! Yes, I shall see him, not as a stranger, but as a friend! What a glorious hope!

The Living Bible

1 CORINTHIANS 15:35-44

But someone may ask, "How are the dead raised? With what kind of body will they come?" How foolish! What you sow does not come to life unless it dies. When you sow, you do not plant the body that will be, but just a seed, perhaps of wheat or of something else. But God gives it a body as he has determined, and to each kind of seed he gives its own body. All flesh is not the same: Men have one kind of flesh, animals have another, birds another and fish another. There are also heavenly bodies and there are earthly bodies; but the splendor of the heavenly bodies is one kind, and the splendor of the earthly bodies is another. The sun has one kind of splendor, the moon another and the stars another; and star differs from star in splendor.

So it will be with the resurrection of the dead. The body that is sown is perishable, it is raised imperishable; it is sown in dishonor, it is raised in glory; it is sown in weakness, it is raised in power; it is sown a natural body, it is raised a spiritual body.

New International Version

GLOSSARY OF TERMS

anatomical gift—the donation of organs for transplant to a living person. If so designated, the entire body or any of its parts can be left to medical research.

autopsy—the medical examination of a dead body. Usually the cadaver is partially or completely dissected.

bier—a bed on which a body is carried to the cemetery.

bi-unit pricing—pricing in which the funeral home divides its price into two figures: one states professional services, the second shows cost of casket.

casket—a box or chest used for viewing and burial of the deceased.

columbarium—an above-ground building in which cremated remains are kept.

concrete boxes—containers that protect the casket from caving in but do not seal off water.

co-op burial—burial by an organization which must declare a dividend and return 20 percent of the profit to the consumer.

cosmetology—the restoration of the appearance of the deceased.

cremains—the remains after cremation.

cremation—the use of intense heat to reduce a body to ashes and bones.

crypt—a concrete chamber in a mausoleum, into which a casket is placed. The chamber is slightly larger than a casket.

disinter—to retrieve a body from the grave.

disposition—final placement or disposal of a dead person.

embalmer—a person who through education and training is licensed to prepare bodies for funerals and burials.

embalming—providing preservation of a body and possible protection against spread of disease.

endowment care—money set aside to pay for the upkeep of a cemetery.

endowment marker care—money set aside to pay for the upkeep of a marker or monument.

exhume—to retrieve a body from the grave.

functional pricing—divides the costs into three large sections: motor equipment, facilities and equipment, and professional services. Each section has a short description and price. Casket is listed separately.

funeral director—someone who serves the public in any aspect of funeral service. Approximately 75 percent of all persons licensed in funeral service hold both a funeral director's and an embalmer's license.

grave liner—a concrete container into which a casket or urn is placed for ground burial. Its function is to prevent the ground from settling.

honorarium—payment for professional services, particularly to clergymen.

interment—placement of a body in a grave.

inurnment—opening and closing of a niche, including the placement and sealing of an urn within.

mausoleum—a building for entombment of the dead.

memorial funds—money donated to an organization in honor of the deceased at the time of death.

memorial parks—cemeteries that require all markers, whether bronze or stone, to be level with the grass.

memorial society—a group of people who have joined together to offer economical funerals. They use the services of a funeral director.

memorials—monuments or other tangible reminders of the deceased.

monument cemeteries—cemeteries which allow traditional monuments. Most of them also permit the burial without monument.

niche—a chamber in a columbarium, into which an urn is placed.

pathologist—a specially trained doctor who investigates the changes in body tissues. In an autopsy he attempts to determine the cause of death or the effects of a disease. A forensic pathologist specializes in criminal deaths.

pre-arrangements—establishing one's choice of casket, cemetery or other preferences before death. This may or may not include paying for the funeral.

pre-funding—making arrangements to pay for a funeral before death.

pulverization—reducing the bones of a cremated body to powder before they can be strewn or scattered.

scattering—the spreading of cremated remains over land or sea; allowed in most areas.

single-unit pricing—the quoting of one figure representing the total charge for a funeral.

state funeral board—the governing, licensing, and inspecting board in most states.

urn—a vase or other vessel to hold the remains after a cremation.

urn (garden)—cemetery plots in which cremated remains are buried.

vault—a container into which the casket is placed. The vault is then usually sealed closed.

viewing—a visitation period with an open casket, allowing friends and relatives to see the deceased's body.

FURTHER READING

Public Documents

Federal Trade Commission, *Survey of Funeral Prices in the District of Columbia,* n.d.

Federal Trade Commission, *Report of the Presiding Officer on Proposed Trade Regulation Rule Concerning Funeral Industry Practices,* Jack E. Kahn, July 1977.

Seattle Regional Office of Federal Trade Commission, *The Price of Death: A Survey Method and Consumer Guide for Funerals, Cemeteries and Grave Markers,* Consumer Survey Handbook 3.

Books

Bayly, Joseph, *The View from a Hearse* (Elgin, Illinois: David C. Cook Publishing Co., 1969).

Grollman, Earl A., *Concerning Death: A Practical Guide for the Living* (Boston: Beacon Press, 1974).

Habonstein, Robert W., *The History of American Funeral Directing* (Milwaukee, Wisconsin: Bulfin Printers, Inc., 1963).

Jackson, Edgar, *The Christian Funeral* (New York: Channel Press, 1966).

Ludwig, Jurgen, *Current Methods of Autopsy Practice* (W. B. Saunders Co., 1972).

Mitford, Jessica, *The American Way of Death* (New York: Simon and Schuster, 1963).

Pine, Vanderlyn R., *Caretaker of the Dead, The American Funeral Director* (New York: Irvington Publishers, Inc., 1975).

Weber, Dudley, *Autopsy Pathology Procedure and Protocol* (Springfield, Illinois: C. C. Thomas, 1973).

Periodicals

American Funeral Director, 1501 Broadway, New York, NY 10036.

Casket and Sunnyside, 274 Madison Avenue, New York, NY 10016.

The Director, 135 West Wells Street, Milwaukee, WI 53203.